TABLE OF CONTENTS

TOP 20 TEST TAKING TIPS 6

THE MATHEMATICS TEST 7
    SOLVING FOR VARIABLES 9
    POSITIVE/NEGATIVE NUMBERS 9
    EXPONENTS 10
    DECIMAL EXPONENTS (AKA SCIENTIFIC NOTATION) 11
    AREA, VOLUME, AND SURFACE AREA 11
    PERCENTS 11
    WORD PROBLEMS 12
    SPECIAL FORMULAS 13
    LINE PLOTTING 15
    SIMPLE PROBABILITY 15
    RATIOS 16
    GRAPHS 16
    TRIGONOMETRY 19
    PLUG AND CHUG 20
    FINAL NOTE 20

THE READING TEST 22
    SKIMMING 23
    PARAGRAPH FOCUS 26
    ELIMINATE CHOICES 27
    CONTEXTUAL CLUES 28
    FACT/OPINION 29
    TIME MANAGEMENT 30
    FINAL WARNINGS 31

THE WRITING SKILLS TEST 33
    SIMPLICITY IS BLISS 35
    PARALLELISM 36
    GRAMMAR TYPE 36
    PUNCTUATION 37
    TENSE 37
    ADDED PHRASES 38

Copyright © Mometrix Media. You have been licensed one copy of this document for personal use only.
Any other reproduction or redistribution is strictly prohibited. All rights reserved.

WORD CONFUSION	38
COMMAS	43
HYPHENS	46
SEMICOLONS	46
PARENTHESES	48
COLON	49
APOSTROPHES	50

THE WRITING ESSAY TEST 52

FINAL NOTE	58

THE SCIENCE TEST 59

THREE TYPES OF PASSAGES	61
FOUR TYPES OF QUESTIONS	62
ANSWER CHOICE ELIMINATION TECHNIQUES	63
TIME MANAGEMENT	66
HIGHLY TECHNICAL QUESTIONS MAY NOT BE	67
EXPERIMENT PASSAGES	68
RANDOM TIPS	68

THE CRITICAL THINKING TEST 70

APPENDIX A: AREA, VOLUME, SURFACE AREA FORMULAS 76

SPECIAL REPORT: CAAP SECRETS IN ACTION 77

SAMPLE QUESTION FROM THE READING TEST:	77
SAMPLE QUESTION FROM THE MATHEMATICS TEST:	81
SAMPLE QUESTION FROM THE ENGLISH TEST:	84
SAMPLE QUESTION FROM THE SCIENCE TEST:	86
SAMPLE TOPIC FOR THE WRITING TEST:	90
SAMPLE QUESTION FROM THE CRITICAL THINKING TEST:	92

SPECIAL REPORT: HOW TO OVERCOME YOUR FEAR OF MATH 95

MATH MYTHS	100
HELPFUL STRATEGIES	102
PAPPAS METHOD	106

SECRET KEY #1 – TIME IS YOUR GREATEST ENEMY 110

Copyright © Mometrix Media. You have been licensed one copy of this document for personal use only. Any other reproduction or redistribution is strictly prohibited. All rights reserved.

    SUCCESS STRATEGY #1 111

SECRET KEY #2 – GUESSING IS NOT GUESSWORK 113

    MONKEYS TAKE THE CAAP 113
    SUCCESS STRATEGY #2 114
    SUMMARY OF GUESSING TECHNIQUES 116

SECRET KEY #3 – PRACTICE SMARTER, NOT HARDER 117

    SUCCESS STRATEGY #3 117

SECRET KEY #4 – PREPARE, DON'T PROCRASTINATE 119

SECRET KEY #5 – TEST YOURSELF 120

    SUCCESS STRATEGY 120

GENERAL STRATEGIES 121

SPECIAL REPORT: ADDITIONAL BONUS MATERIAL 130

Top 20 Test Taking Tips

1. Carefully follow all the test registration procedures
2. Know the test directions, duration, topics, question types, how many questions
3. Setup a flexible study schedule at least 3-4 weeks before test day
4. Study during the time of day you are most alert, relaxed, and stress free
5. Maximize your learning style; visual learner use visual study aids, auditory learner use auditory study aids
6. Focus on your weakest knowledge base
7. Find a study partner to review with and help clarify questions
8. Practice, practice, practice
9. Get a good night's sleep; don't try to cram the night before the test
10. Eat a well balanced meal
11. Know the exact physical location of the testing site; drive the route to the site prior to test day
12. Bring a set of ear plugs; the testing center could be noisy
13. Wear comfortable, loose fitting, layered clothing to the testing center; prepare for it to be either cold or hot during the test
14. Bring at least 2 current forms of ID to the testing center
15. Arrive to the test early; be prepared to wait and be patient
16. Eliminate the obviously wrong answer choices, then guess the first remaining choice
17. Pace yourself; don't rush, but keep working and move on if you get stuck
18. Maintain a positive attitude even if the test is going poorly
19. Keep your first answer unless you are positive it is wrong
20. Check your work, don't make a careless mistake

The Mathematics Test

The CAAP Mathematics Test is a 35-item, 40-minute test designed to measure students' proficiency in mathematical reasoning. The test assesses students' proficiency in solving mathematical problems encountered in many postsecondary curricula. It emphasizes quantitative reasoning rather than the memorization of formulas.

ACT permits the use of calculators on the CAAP Mathematics Test for examinees who wish to use them; however, all problems on the test can be solved without using calculators.

The content areas tested include prealgebra; elementary, intermediate, and advanced algebra; coordinate geometry; and trigonometry. Descriptions of the content areas and the approximate proportions of items in each are provided below.

- **Prealgebra.** Items in this category involve operations with whole numbers, decimals, and fractions; order concepts; percentages; averages; exponents; scientific notation; and similar concepts.

- **Elementary Algebra.** Items in this category involve basic operations with polynomials, setting up equations, and substituting values into algebraic expressions. They may also require the solution of linear equations in one variable and other related topics.

- **Intermediate Algebra.** Items in this category assess students' understanding of exponents, rational expressions, and systems of linear equations. Other concepts such as the quadratic formula and absolute value inequalities may also be tested.

- **Coordinate Geometry.** Knowledge and skills assessed in this category may include graphing in the standard coordinate plane or the real number line, graphing conics, linear equations in two variables, graphing systems of equations, and similar types of skills.

- **College Algebra.** Items in this category are based on advanced algebra concepts including rational exponents, exponential and logarithmic functions, complex numbers, matrices, inverses of functions, and domains and ranges.

- **Trigonometry.** Items in this category include concepts such as right triangle trigonometry, graphs of trigonometric functions, basic trigonometric identities, and trigonometric equations and inequalities.

Three scores are reported for the CAAP Mathematics Test:
1. a total test score based on all 35 items
2. a subscore in Basic Algebra based on 17 items
3. a subscore in College Algebra based on the remaining 18 items

The Basic Algebra subscore is composed of test questions from the prealgebra, elementary algebra, intermediate algebra, and coordinate geometry content areas. The College Algebra subscore is composed of test questions from the College Algebra and Trigonometry content areas.

A detailed knowledge of algebra and trigonometry is NOT necessary to answer to succeed on CAAP Mathematics test. Don't be intimidated by the questions presented. They do not require highly advanced math knowledge, but only the ability to recognize basic problems types and apply simple formulas and methods to solving them.

That is our goal, to show you the simple formulas and methods to solving these problems, so that while you will not gain a mastery of math from this guide, you will learn the methods necessary to succeed on the CAAP. This guide attacks problems that are simple in nature but may have been glossed over during your education.

- All numbers used are real numbers.
- Figures or drawings beside questions are provided as additional information that should be useful in solving the problem. They are drawn fairly accurately, unless the figure is noted as "not drawn to scale".
- Jagged or straight lines can both be assumed to be straight.
- Unless otherwise stated, all drawings and figures lie in a plane.

Solving for Variables

Variables are letters that represent an unknown number. You must solve what that number is in single variable problems. The main thing to remember is that you can do anything to one side of an equation as long as you do it to the other.

Example: Solve for x in the equation $2x + 3 = 5$.
Answer: First you want to get the "2x" isolated by itself on one side. To do that, first get rid of the 3. Subtract 3 from both sides of the equation $2x + 3 - 3 = 5 - 3$ or $2x = 2$. Now since the x is being multiplied by the 2 in "2x", you must divide by 2 to get rid of it. So, divide both sides by 2, which gives $2x / 2 = 2 / 2$ or $x = 1$.

Positive/Negative Numbers

Multiplication/Division

A negative multiplied or divided by a negative = a positive number.
Example: $-3 * -4 = 12$; $-6 / -3 = 2$

A negative multiplied by a positve = a negative number.

Example: -3 * 4 = -12; -6 / 3 = -2

Addition/Subtraction

Treat a negative sign just like a subtraction sign.

Example: 3 + -2 = 3 − 2 or 1

Remember that you can reverse the numbers while adding or subtracting.

Example: -4+2 = 2 + -4 = 2 − 4 = -2

A negative number subtracted from another number is the same as adding a positive number.

Example: 2 - -1 = 2 + 1 = 3

Beware of making a simple mistake!

Example: An outdoor thermometer drops from 42° to − 8°. By how many degrees has the outside air cooled?

Answer: A common mistake is to say 42° − 8° = 34°, but that is wrong. It is actually 42° - - 8° or 42° + 8° = 50°

Exponents

When exponents are multiplied together, the exponents are added to get the final result.

Example: $x*x = x^2$, where x^1 is implied and 1 + 1 = 2.

When exponents in parentheses have an exponent, the exponents are multiplied to get the final result.

Example: $(x^3)^2 = x^6$, because 3*2 = 6.

Another way to think of this is that $(x^3)^2$ is the same as $(x^3)*(x^3)$. Now you can use the multiplication rule given above and add the exponents, 3 + 3 = 6, so $(x^3)^2 = x^6$

Decimal Exponents (AKA Scientific Notation)

This usually involves converting back and forth between scientific notation and decimal numbers (e.g. 0.02 is the same as 2×10^{-2}). There's an old "cheat" to this problem: if the number is less than 1, the number of digits behind the decimal point is the same as the exponent that 10 is raised to in scientific notation, except that the exponent is a negative number; if the number is greater than 1, the exponent of 10 is equal to the number of digits ahead of the decimal point minus 1.

Example: Convert 3000 to decimal notation.

Answer: 3×10^3, since 4 digits are ahead of the decimal, the number is greater than 1, and (4-1) = 3.

Example: Convert 0.05 to decimal notation.

Answer: 5×10^{-2}, since the five is two places behind the decimal (remember, the exponent is negative for numbers less than 1).

Any number raised to an exponent of zero is always 1. Also, unless you know what you're doing, always convert scientific notation to "regular" decimal numbers before doing arithmetic, and convert the answer back if necessary to answer the problem.

Area, Volume, and Surface Area

You can count on questions about area, volume, and surface area to be a significant part of the CAAP. Your best bet is to just memorize the formulas for test day. A list is provided in the appendix for your convenience.

Percents

A percent can be converted to a decimal simply by dividing it by 100.

Example: What is 2% of 50?

Answer: 2% = 2/100 or .02, so .02 * 50 = 1

Word Problems

Some word problems involve percents.

Example: Ticket sales for this year's annual concert at Minutemaid Park were $125,000. The promoter is predicting that next year's sales, in dollars, will be 40% greater than this year's. How many dollars in ticket sales is the promoter predicting for next year?

Answer: Next year's is 40% greater. 40% = 40/100 = .4, so .4 * $125,000 = $50,000. However, the example stated that next year's would be greater by that amount, so next year's sales would be this year's at $125,000 plus the increase at $50,000. $125,000 + $50,000 = $175,000

Some word problems involve distances.

Example: In a certain triangle, the longest side is 1 foot longer than the second-longest side, and the second-longest side is 1 foot longer than the shortest side. If the perimeter is 30 feet, how many feet long is the shortest side.

Answer: There are three sides, let's call them A, B, and C. A is the longest, B the medium sized, and C the shortest. Because A is described in reference to B's length and B is described in reference to C's length, all calculations should be done off of C, the final reference. Use a variable to represent C's length, "x". This means that C is "x" long, B is "x + 1" because B was 1 foot longer than C, and A is "x + 1 + 1" because A was 1 foot longer than B. To calculate a perimeter you simply add all three sides together, so P = length A + length B + length C, or (x) + (x + 1) + (x + 1 + 1) = x + x + x + 1 + 1 + 1 = 3x + 3. You know that the perimeter equals 30 feet, so 3x + 3 = 30. Subtracting 3 from both sides gives 3x + 3 − 3 = 30 − 3 or 3x = 27. Dividing both sides by 3 to get "x" all by itself gives 3x / 3 = 27 / 3 or x = 9. So C = x = 9, and B = x + 1 = 9 + 1 = 10, and
A = x + 1 + 1 = 9 + 1 + 1 = 11. A quick check of 9 + 10 + 11 = 30 for the perimeter distance proves that the answer of x = 9 is correct

Some word problems involve ratios.

Example: An architect is drawing a scaled blueprint of an apartment building that is to be 100 feet wide and 250 feet long. On the drawing, if the building is 25 inches long, how many inches wide should it be.

Answer: Recognize the word "scaled" to indicate a similar drawing. Similar drawings or shapes can be solved using ratios. First, create the ratio fraction for the missing number, in this case the number of inches wide the drawing should be. The numerator of the first ratio fraction will be the matching known side, in this case "100 feet" wide. The question "100 feet wide is to how many inches wide?" gives us the first fraction of 100 / x. The question "250 feet long is to 25 inches long?" gives us the second fraction of 250 / 25. Again, note that both numerators (100 and 250) are from the same shape. The denominators ("x" and 25) are both from the same shape or drawing as well. Cross multiplication gives 100 * 25 = 250 * x or 2500 = 250x. Dividing both sides by 250 to get x by itself yields 2500 / 250 = 250x / 250 or 10 = x.

Special Formulas

FOIL (First, Outer, Inner, Last)

When you are given a problem such as $(x + 2)(x - 3)$, you should use the FOIL method of multiplication. First, multiply the First parts of each equation (x*x). Then multiply the Outer parts of each equation (x*-3). Note that you should treat the minus 3 in the second equation as a negative 3. Then multiply the Inner parts of each equation (2*x). Finally, multiply the Last parts of each equation (2*-3). Once you are finished, add each part together $(x*x)+(x*-3)+(2*x)+(2*-3) = x^2 + -3x + 2x + -6 = x^2 - 3x + 2x - 6 = x^2 - 1x - 6 = x^2 - x - 6$.

Slope-Intercept formula

$y = mx + b$, where m is the slope of the line and b is the y-intercept.

Example: In the (x,y) coordinate plane, what is the slope of the line $2y = x - 4$?

Answer: First this needs to be converted into slope intercept form. Divide both sides by 2, which gives $2y/2 = (x-4)/2$ or $y = x/2 - 2$. $x/2$ is the same as $½ *x$, so since m in the formula $y = mx+b$ is the slope, then in the equation $y = ½ * x - 2$, $½$ is the slope.

Example: In the (x,y) coordinate plane, where does the line $y = 2x - 3$ cross the y-axis?

Answer: In the formula $y = mx + b$, b is the y – intercept, or where the line crosses the y-axis. In this case, b is represented by –3, so –3 is where the line crosses the y-axis.

Example: In the (x, y) coordinate plane, what is the slope of the line $y = x + 2$?

Answer: This is already in the slope intercept form of $y = mx + b$. Whenever x does not have a number in front of it, you can always assume that there is a 1 there. Therefore, this equation could also be written as $y = 1x + 2$, which means $m = 1$, and the slope is 1.

Slope formula

$m = (y1 - y2)/(x1 - x2)$, where m is the slope of the line and two points on the line are given by (x1,y1) and (x2,y2). This can sometimes be remembered by the statement "rise over run", which means that the "y" values represent the "rise" as they are the up and down dimension and the "x" values represent the "run" as they are the side to side dimension.

Example: What is the slope of a line that passes through points (5,1) and (-2, 3).

Answer: $m = (y1 - y2)/(x1 - x2)$ or $(1 - 3)/(5 - -2)$ or $-2 / (5 + 2)$ or $-2 / 7$

Line Plotting

If you are trying to plot a line, there is an easy way to do it. First convert the line into slope intercept form (y = mx + b). Then, put a dot on the y-axis at the value of b. For example, if you have a line given by y= 2/3x + 1, then the first point on the line would be at (0,1), because 1 is the y-intercept, or where the line crosses the y-axis. To find the next point on the line, use the slope, which is 2/3. First go 2 increments up, and then 3 increments to the right. To find the next point on the line, go 2 more increments up, and then 3 more increments to the right. You should always go either up or down depending on the numerator in the slope fraction. So if the slope is 3/5, then the numerator is 3, and you should go 3 increments up and 5 increments to the right. You should always go to the right the amount of the denominator. So if the slope is –2, then first you should remember that –2 is the same as –2/1. Since –2 is the denominator, you should go down 2 increments and then 1 increment to the right.

Remember that positive slopes slope upward from left to right and that negative slopes slope downward from left to right.

Simple Probability

The probability problems on the ACT are fairly straightforward. The basic idea is this: the probability that something will happen is the number of possible ways that something can happen divided by the total number of possible ways for all things that can happen.

Example: I have 20 balloons, 12 are red, 8 are yellow. I give away one yellow balloon; if the next balloon is randomly picked, what is the probability that it will be yellow?

Answer: The probability is 7/19, because after giving one away, there are 7 different ways that the "something" can happen, divided 19 remaining possibilities.

Ratios

When a question asks about two similar shapes, expect a ratio problem.

Example: The figure below shows 2 triangles, where triangle ABC ~ A'B'C'. In these similar triangles, a = 3, b = 4, c = 5, and a' = 6. What is the value of b'?

Answer: You are given the dimensions of 1 side that is similar on both triangles (a and a'). You are looking for b' and are given the dimensions of b. Therefore you can set up a ratio of a/a' = b/b' or 3/6 = 4/b'. To solve, cross multiply the two sides, multiplying 6*4 = 3*b' or 24 = 3b'. Dividing both sides by 3 (24/3 = 3b'/3) makes 8 = b', so 8 is the answer.

Note many other problems may have opportunities to use a ratio. Look for problems where you are trying to find dimensions for a shape and you have dimensions for a similar shape. These can nearly always be solved by setting up a ratio. Just be careful and set up corresponding measurements in the ratios. First decide what you are being asked for on shape B, represented by a variable, such as x. Then ask yourself, which side on similar A is the same size side as x. That is your first ratio fraction, set up a fraction like 2/x if 2 is the similar size side on shape A. Then find a side on each shape that is similar. If 4 is the size of another side on shape A and it corresponds to a side with size 3 on shape B, then your second ratio fraction is 4/3. Note that 2 and 4 are the two numerators in the ratio fractions and are both from shape A. Also note that "x" the unknown side and 3 are both the denominators in the ratio fractions and are both from shape B.

Graphs

Midpoints

To find a midpoint, find the difference in the x-direction between the two endpoints given, and divide by two. Then add that number to the leftmost endpoint's x coordinate. That will be the x coordinate of the midpoint. Next find the difference in the y-direction between the two endpoints given, and divide by two. Then add that number to the lower endpoint's y coordinate. That will be the y coordinate of the midpoint.

Example: What is the midpoint of the line segment with endpoints of (-2 , 5) and (4 , 1)?

Answer: First, subtract the leftmost endpoint's x coordinate from the rightmost endpoint's x coordinate 4 - -2 = 4 + 2 = 6. Then divide by two, 6 / 2 = 3. Then add that number to the leftmost x coordinate -2 + 3 = 1, which is the midpoint's x coordinate. Second, subtract the lower endpoint's y coordinate from the higher endpoint's y coordinate 5 – 1 = 4. Then divide by two, 4 / 2 = 2. Then add that number to the lower y coordinate 1 + 2 = 3, which is the midpoint's y coordinate. So the midpoint is given by (1 , 3).

Angles

If you have a two intersecting lines, remember that the sum of all of the angles can only be 360°. In fact, the two angles on either side of each line will add up to 180°. In the example below, on either side of each line, there is a 137° angle and a 43° angle (137° + 43°) = 180°. Also note that opposite angles are equal. For example, the 43° angle is matched by a similar 43° angle on the opposite side of the intersection.

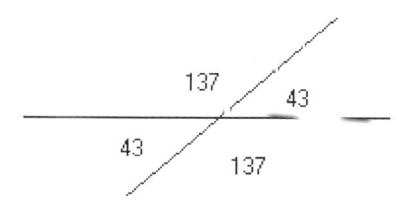

Additionally, parallel lines intersected by a third line will share angles. In the example below, note how each 128° angle is matched by a 128° angle on the opposite side. Also, all of the other angles in this example are 52° angles, because all of the angles on one side of a line have to equal 180° and since there are only two angles, if you have the degree of one, then you can find the degree of the other. In this case, the missing angle is given by 180° − 128° = 52°.

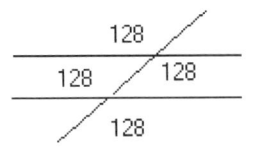

```
         128
    128  /  128
         /
        128
```

Finally, remember that all of the angles in a triangle will add up to 180°. If you are given two of the angles, then subtract them both from 180° and you will have the degree of the third missing angle.

Example: If you have a triangle with two given angles of 20° and 130°, what degree is the third angle?

Answer: All angles must add up to 180°, so 180° − 20° − 130° = 30°.

Right Triangles

Whenever you see the words "right triangle" or "90° angle," alarm bells should go off. These problems will almost always involve the law of right triangles, AKA The Pythagorean Theorem:

$A^2 + B^2 = C^2$

Where A = the length of one of the shorter sides

B = the length of the other shorter side

C = the length of the hypotenuse or longest side opposite the 90° angle

MAKE SURE YOU KNOW THIS FORMULA. At least 3-5 questions will reference variations on this formula by giving you two of the three variables and asking you to solve for the third.

Example: A right triangle has sides of 3 and 4; what is the length of the hypotenuse?

Answer: Solving the equation, $A^2=9$, $B^2=16$, so $C^2=25$; the square root of 25 is 5, the length of the hypotenuse C.

Example: In the rectangle below, what is the length of the diagonal line?

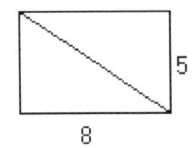

```
 _____
|       /|
|      / | 5
|     /  |
|____/___|
    8
```

Answer: This rectangle is actually made of two right triangles. Whenever you have a right triangle, the Pythagorean Theorem can be used. Since the right side of the triangle is equal to 5, then the left side must also be equal to 5. This creates a triangle with one side equal to 5 and another side equal to 8. To use the Pythagorean Theorem, we state that $5^2 + 8^2 = C^2$ or $25 + 64 = C^2$ or $89 = C^2$ or C = Square Root of 89

Circles

Many students have never seen the formula for a circle:

$(x-A)^2 + (y-B)^2 = r^2$

This looks intimidating, but it's really not:

A = the coordinate of the center on the x-axis

B = the coordinate of the center on the y-axis

r = the radius of the circle

Example: What is the radius of the circle described by: $(x+2)^2 + (x-3)^2 = 16$

Answer: Since $r^2 = 16$, r, the radius, equals 4.

Also, this circle is centered at (-2,3) since those must be the values of A and B in the generic equation to make it the same as this equation.

Trigonometry

There are three basic formulas that should be remembered. ALL trigonometry problems on the ACT can be solved using only these formulas.

1.) SOHCAHTOA: Sin = Opposite / Hypotenuse; Cosine = Adjacent / Hypotenuse; Tangent = Opposite / Adjacent

   Opposite refers to the opposite side of the triangle from the referenced angle.

   Adjacent refers to the adjacent side of the triangle from the referenced angle.

   Hypotenuse refers to the longest side of the triangle.

2.) $Sin^2 + Cos^2 = 1$

Sometimes you will see this written differently: $Cos^2 = 1 - Sin^2$; $Sin^2 = 1 - Cos^2$; $Cos^2 - 1 = -Sin^2$

3.) $Sin / Cos = Tan$

Sometimes this will be written differently: $Sin = Cos * Tan$; $Cos = Sin / Tan$; $Sin^2/Cos^2 = Tan^2$

Example: What is another way of writing $2 \cos\theta * \sin\theta$?

Answer: $Sin\theta = Cos\theta * Tan\theta$, so it could be rewritten as $2 * \cos\theta * (\cos\theta * \tan\theta)$ or $2 * \cos^2\theta * \tan\theta$.

Note: Do not get thrown off by Greek letters after the word Sin, Cos, or Tan. Sometimes you might see $Sin\theta$, $Sin\alpha$, or $Sin\beta$. Just ignore the Greek letters, they won't affect the problem, so pretend they are not there. Just solve the problem without worrying about them.

Plug and Chug

Sometimes when faced by a problem containing variables that are confusing, replace the variables with some made up numbers, then test those numbers with your calculator to come up with an answer.

Sometimes you can also plug each of the answer choices in and see which one is right. Let your calculator work for you.

Final Note

As mentioned before, word problems describing shapes should always be drawn out. Remember the old adage that a picture is worth a thousand words. If geometric shapes are described (line segments, circles, squares, etc) draw them out rather than trying to visualize how they should look.

Approach problems systematically. Take time to understand what is being asked for. In many cases there is a drawing or graph that you can write on. Draw lines, jot notes, do whatever is necessary to create a visual picture and to allow you to understand what is being asked.

Even if you have always done well in math, you may not succeed on the CAAP. While math tests in school test specific competencies in specific subjects, the CAAP frequently tests your ability to apply math concepts from vastly different math subjects in one problem. However, in few cases is any CAAP Mathematics problem more than two "layers" deep.

What does this mean for you? You can easily learn the CAAP Mathematics through taking multiple practice tests. If you have some gaps in your math knowledge, we suggest you buy a more basic study guide to help you build a foundation before applying our secrets.

The Reading Test

The CAAP Reading Test is a 36-item, 40-minute test that measures reading comprehension as a combination of skills that can be conceptualized in two broad categories: Referring Skills and Reasoning Skills.

- **Referring Skills.** Test items that focus on referring skills require the student to derive meaning from text by identifying and interpreting specific information that is explicitly stated. Typical items of this type require students to recognize main ideas of paragraphs and passages, to identify important factual information, and to identify relationships among different components of textual information.

- **Reasoning Skills.** Test items that focus on reasoning skills require students to determine implicit meanings and to go beyond the information that is explicitly presented. Typical items in this category assess students' ability to determine meaning from context, to infer main ideas and relationships, to generalize and apply information beyond the immediate context, to draw appropriate conclusions, and to make appropriate comparisons.

The Reading Test consists of four prose passages of about 900 words each that are representative of the level and kinds of writing commonly encountered in college curricula. The four reading passages come from the following four content areas, one passage from each area:

- Prose Fiction—Entire stories or excerpts from short stories or novels.

- Humanities—Art, music, philosophy, theater, architecture, or dance.

- Social Studies—History, political science, economics, anthropology, psychology, or sociology.

☐ Natural Sciences—Biology, chemistry, physics, or the physical sciences.
Each passage is accompanied by a set of nine multiple-choice test items that focus on the set of complementary and mutually supportive skills that readers must use in studying written materials across a range of subject areas.

Three Reading scores are reported:
1. a total test score based on all 36 items
2. a subscore in Arts/Literature based on 18 items in Prose Fiction and Humanities
3. a subscore in Social Studies/Sciences based on 18 items in the Social Studies and Natural Science

Skimming

Your first task when you begin reading is to answer the question "What is the topic of the selection?" This can best be answered by quickly skimming the passage for the general idea, stopping to read only the first sentence of each paragraph. A paragraph's first is usually the main topic sentence, and it gives you a summary of the content of the paragraph.

Once you've skimmed the passage, stopping to read only the first sentences, you will have a general idea about what it is about, as well as what is the expected topic in each paragraph.

Each question will contain clues as to where to find the answer in the passage. Do not just randomly search through the passage for the correct answer to each question. Search scientifically. Find key word(s) or ideas in the question that are going to either contain or be near the correct answer. These are typically nouns, verbs, numbers, or phrases in the question that will probably be duplicated in the passage. Once you have identified those key word(s) or idea, skim the passage quickly to find where those key word(s) or idea appears. The correct answer choice will be nearby.

Example: What caused Martin to suddenly return to Paris?

The key word is Paris. Skim the passage quickly to find where this word appears. The answer will be close by that word.

However, sometimes key words in the question are not repeated in the passage. In those cases, search for the general idea of the question.

Example: Which of the following was the psychological impact of the author's childhood upon the remainder of his life?

Key words are "childhood" or "psychology". While searching for those words, be alert for other words or phrases that have similar meaning, such as "emotional effect" or "mentally" which could be used in the passage, rather than the exact word "psychology".

Numbers or years can be particularly good key words to skim for, as they stand out from the rest of the text.

Example: Which of the following best describes the influence of Monet's work in the 20th century?

20th contains numbers and will easily stand out from the rest of the text. Use 20th as the key word to skim for in the passage.

Other good key word(s) may be in quotation marks. These identify a word or phrase that is copied directly from the passage. In those cases, the word(s) in quotation marks are exactly duplicated in the passage.

Example: In her college years, what was meant by Margaret's "drive for excellence"?

"Drive for excellence" is a direct quote from the passage and should be easy to find.

Once you've quickly found the correct section of the passage to find the answer, focus upon the answer choices. Sometimes a choice will repeat word for word a portion of the passage near the answer. However, beware of such duplication – it may be a trap! More than likely, the correct choice will paraphrase or summarize the related portion of the passage, rather than being exactly the same wording.

For the answers that you think are correct, read them carefully and make sure that they answer the question. An answer can be factually correct, but it MUST answer the question asked. Additionally, two answers can both be seemingly correct, so be sure to read all of the answer choices, and make sure that you get the one that BEST answers the question.

Some questions will not have a key word.

Example: Which of the following would the author of this passage likely agree with?

In these cases, look for key words in the answer choices. Then skim the passage to find where the answer choice occurs. By skimming to find where to look, you can minimize the time required.

Sometimes it may be difficult to identify a good key word in the question to skim for in the passage. In those cases, look for a key word in one of the answer choices to skim for. Often the answer choices can all be found in the same paragraph, which can quickly narrow your search.

Paragraph Focus

Focus upon the first sentence of each paragraph, which is the most important. The main topic of the paragraph is usually there.

Once you've read the first sentence in the paragraph, you have a general idea about what each paragraph will be about. As you read the questions, try to determine which paragraph will have the answer. Paragraphs have a concise topic. The answer should either obviously be there or obviously not. It will save time if you can jump straight to the paragraph, so try to remember what you learned from the first sentences.

Example: The first paragraph is about poets; the second is about poetry. If a question asks about poetry, where will the answer be? The second paragraph.

The main idea of a passage is typically spread across all or most of its paragraphs. Whereas the main idea of a paragraph may be completely different than the main idea of the very next paragraph, a main idea for a passage affects all of the paragraphs in one form or another.

Example: What is the main idea of the passage?

For each answer choice, try to see how many paragraphs are related. It can help to count how many sentences are affected by each choice, but it is best to see how many paragraphs are affected by the choice. Typically the answer choices will include incorrect choices that are main ideas of individual paragraphs, but not the entire passage. That is why it is crucial to choose ideas that are supported by the most paragraphs possible.

Eliminate Choices

Some choices can quickly be eliminated. "Andy Warhol lived there." Is Andy Warhol even mentioned in the article? If not, quickly eliminate it.

When trying to answer a question such as "the passage indicates all of the following EXCEPT" quickly skim the paragraph searching for references to each choice. If the reference exists, scratch it off as a choice. Similar choices may be crossed off simultaneously if they are close enough.

In choices that ask you to choose "which answer choice does NOT describe?" or "all of the following answer choices are identifiable characteristics, EXCEPT which?" look for answers that are similarly worded. Since only one answer can be correct, if there are two answers that appear to mean the same thing, they must BOTH be incorrect, and can be eliminated.

Example:

A.) changing values and attitudes

B.) a large population of mobile or uprooted people

These answer choices are similar; they both describe a fluid culture. Because of their similarity, they can be linked together. Since the answer can have only one choice, they can also be eliminated together.

When presented with a question that offers two choices, or neither choice, or both choice, it is rarely both choices.

Example: When an atom emits a beta particle, the mass of the atom will:
- A. increase
- B. decrease.
- C. stay the same.
- D. either increase or decrease depending on conditions.
- E. neither increase or decrease

Answer D and E will rarely be correct, the answers are usually more concrete.

Contextual Clues

Look for contextual clues. An answer can be right but not correct. The contextual clues will help you find the answer that is most right and is correct. Understand the context in which a phrase is stated.

When asked for the implied meaning of a statement made in the passage, immediately go find the statement and read the context it was made in. Also, look for an answer choice that has a similar phrase to the statement in question.
Example: In the passage, what is implied by the phrase "Churches have become more or less part of the furniture"?

Find an answer choice that is similar or describes the phrase "part of the furniture" as that is the key phrase in the question. "Part of the furniture" is a saying that means something is fixed, immovable, or set in their ways. Those are all similar ways of saying "part of the furniture." As such, the correct answer choice will probably include a similar rewording of the expression.

Example: Why was John described as "morally desperate".

The answer will probably have some sort of definition of morals in it. "Morals" refers to a code of right and wrong behavior, so the correct answer choice will likely have words that mean something like that.

Fact/Opinion

When asked about which statement is a fact or opinion, remember that answer choices that are facts will typically have no ambiguous words. For example, how long is a long time? What defines an ordinary person? These ambiguous words of "long" and "ordinary" should not be in a factual statement. However, if all of the choices have ambiguous words, go to the context of the passage. Often a factual statement may be set out as a research finding.

Example: "The scientist found that the eye reacts quickly to change in light."

Opinions may be set out in the context of words like thought, believed, understood, or wished.

Example: "He thought the Yankees should win the World Series."

Opposites

Answer choices that are direct opposites are usually correct. The paragraph will often contain established relationships (when this goes up, that goes down). The question may ask you to draw conclusions for this and will give two similar answer choices that are opposites.

Example:

A.) if other factors are held constant, then increasing the interest rate will lead to a decrease in housing starts

B.) if other factors are held constant, then increasing the interest rate will lead to an increase in housing starts

Often these opposites will not be so clearly recognized. Don't be thrown off by different wording, look for the meaning beneath. Notice how these two answer choices are really opposites, with just a slight change in the wording shown above. Once you realize these are opposites, you should examine them closely. One of these two is likely to be the correct answer.

Example:

A.) if other factors are held constant, then increasing the interest rate will lead to a decrease in housing starts

B.) when there is an increase in housing starts, and other things remaining equal, it is often the result of an increase in interest rates

Answer the Question

It may seem obvious to only pick answer choices that answer the question, but CAAP can create some excellent answer choices that are wrong. Don't pick an answer just because it sounds right, or you believe it to be true. It MUST answer the question. Once you've made your selection, always go back and check it against the question and make sure that you didn't misread the question, and the answer choice does answer the question posed.

Time Management

In technical passages, do not get lost on the technical terms. Skip them and move on. You want a general understanding of what is going on, not a mastery of the passage.

When you encounter material in the selection that seems difficult to understand, it often may not be necessary and can be skipped. Only spend time trying to understand it if it is going to be relevant for a question. Understand difficult phrases only as a last resort.

Answer general questions before detail questions. A reader with a good understanding of the whole passage can often answer general questions without rereading a word. Get the easier questions out of the way before tackling the more time consuming ones.

Identify each question by type. Usually the wording of a question will tell you whether you can find the answer by referring directly to the passage or by using your reasoning powers. You alone know which question types you customarily handle with ease and which give you trouble and will require more time. Save the difficult questions for last.

Final Warnings

Hedge Phrases Revisited

Once again, watch out for critical "hedge" phrases, such as likely, may, can, will often, sometimes, etc, often, almost, mostly, usually, generally, rarely, sometimes. Question writers insert these hedge phrases, to cover every possibility. Often an answer will be wrong simply because it leaves no room for exception.
Example: Animals live longer in cold places than animals in warm places.

This answer choice is wrong, because there are exceptions in which certain warm climate animals live longer. This answer choice leaves no possibility of exception. It states that every animal species in cold places live longer than animal species in warm places. Correct answer choices will typically have a key hedge word to leave room for exceptions.
Example: In severe cold, a polar bear cub is likely to survive longer than an adult polar bear.

This answer choice is correct, because not only does the passage imply that younger animals survive better in the cold, it also allows for exceptions to exist. The use of the word "likely" leaves room for cases in which a polar bear cub might not survive longer than the adult polar bear.

Word Usage Questions

When asked how a word is used in the passage, don't use your existing knowledge of the word. The question is being asked precisely because there is some strange or unusual usage of the word in the passage. Go to the passage and use contextual clues to determine the answer. Don't simply use the popular definition you already know.

Switchback Words

Stay alert for "switchbacks". These are the words and phrases frequently used to alert you to shifts in thought. The most common switchback word is "but". Others include although, however, nevertheless, on the other hand, even though, while, in spite of, despite, regardless of.

Avoid "Fact Traps"

Once you know which paragraph the answer will be in, focus on that paragraph. However, don't get distracted by a choice that is factually true about the paragraph. Your search is for the answer that answers the question, which may be about a tiny aspect in the paragraph. Stay focused and don't fall for an answer that describes the larger picture of the paragraph. Always go back to the question and make sure you're choosing an answer that actually answers the question and is not just a true statement.

[Handwritten annotations: "Revised Plan. Develop", "15 hrs online", "10 hrs writing / CAPP", "Save copies."]

The Writing Skills Test

[Handwritten: "60 minutes extended Time."]

The CAAP Writing Skills Test is a 72-item, 40-minute test measuring students' understanding of the conventions of standard written English in punctuation, grammar, sentence structure, strategy, organization, and style. Spelling, vocabulary, and rote recall of rules of grammar are not tested.

The test consists of six prose passages, each of which is accompanied by a set of 12 multiple-choice test items. A range of passage types is used to provide a variety of rhetorical situations.

Three CAAP Writing Skills scores are reported:
1. a total test score based on all 72 items
2. a subscore in Usage/Mechanics based on the 32 punctuation, grammar, and sentence structure items
3. a subscore in Rhetorical Skills based on the 40 organization, strategy, and style items

Usage/Mechanics. Items that measure usage and mechanics offer alternative responses, including "NO CHANGE," to underlined portions of the text. The student must decide which alternative employs the conventional practice in usage and mechanics that best fits the context.

▪ Punctuation. Use and placement of commas, colons, semicolons, dashes, parentheses, apostrophes, and quotation, question, and exclamation marks.

▪ Grammar. Adjectives and adverbs, conjunctions, and agreement between subject and verb and between pronouns and their antecedents.

- Sentence structure. Relationships between/among clauses, placement of modifiers, and shifts in construction.

Rhetorical Skills. Items that measure rhetorical skills may refer to an underlined portion of the text or may ask a question about a section of the passage or about the passage as a whole. The student must decide which alternative response is most appropriate in a given rhetorical situation.

- Organization. Organization of ideas and relevance of statements in context (order, coherence, unity).

- Strategy. Appropriateness of expression in relation to audience and purpose, strengthening of writing with appropriate supporting material, and effective choice of statements of theme and purpose.

- Style. Precision and appropriateness in the choice of words and images, rhetorically effective management of sentence elements, avoidance of ambiguous pronoun references, and economy in writing.

The Writing Skills portion of the CAAP will have questions about underlined portions of text, with possible replacements as answer choices. Read the text four times, each time replacing the underlined portion with one of the choices. While reading the choices, read the sentence before, the sentence containing, and the sentence after the underlined portion. Sometimes an answer may make sense until you read the following sentence and see how the two sentences flow together. While reading the text, be sure to pause at each comma. If the comma is necessary the pause will be logical. If the comma is not needed, then the sentence will feel awkward. Transitional words should create smooth, logical transitions and maintain a constant flow of text.

Some questions will be concerning sentence insertions. In those cases, do not look for the ones that simply restate what was in the previous sentence. New sentences should contain new information and new insights into the subject of the text. If asked for the paragraph to which a sentence would most naturally be added, find a key noun or word in that new sentence. Then find the paragraph containing exactly or another word closely related to that key noun or word. That is the paragraph that should include the new sentence.

Some questions will ask what purpose a phrase fulfilled in a particular text. It depends upon the subject of the text. If the text is dramatic, then the phrase was probably used to show drama. If the text is comedic, then the phrase was probably to show comedy.

In related cases, you may be asked to provide a sentence that summarizes the text. Simple sentences, without wordy phrases, are usually best. If asked for a succinct answer, then the shorter the answer, the more likely it is correct.

Simplicity is Bliss

Simplicity cannot be overstated. You should never choose a longer, more complicated, or wordier replacement if a simple one will do. When a point can be made with fewer words, choose that answer. However, never sacrifice the flow of text for simplicity. If an answer is simple, but does not make sense, then it is not correct.

Beware of added phrases that don't add anything of meaning, such as "to be" or "as to them". Often these added phrases will occur just before a colon, which may come before a list of items. However, the colon does not need a lengthy introduction. The italics phrases in the below examples are wordy and unnecessary. They should be removed and the colon placed directly after the words "sport" and "following".

Example 1: There are many advantages to running as a sport, *of which the top advantages are*:

Example 2: The school supplies necessary were the following, *of which a few are*:

Parallelism

Often clues to the best answer are given within the text, if you know where to look for them. The correct answer will always be parallel in grammar type, punctuation, format, and tense as the rest of the sentence.

Grammar Type

If a series of nouns is given, then make sure your choice is a noun. If those nouns are plural, then ensure that your choice is plural.

Example: schools, politics, and governments

If a series of verbs is given, then make sure your choice is a verb.
Example: eat, sleep, and drink

If a series of infinitives is given, then make sure your choice is an infinitive.
Example: to trust, to honor, and to obey

If a series of phrases is given, then make sure your choice is a similar phrase.
Example: of controlling, of policing, and of maintaining

Punctuation

If a section of text has an opening dash, parentheses, or comma at the beginning of a phrase, then you can be sure there should be a matching closing dash, parentheses, or comma at the end of the phrase. If items in a series all have commas between them, then any additional items in that series will also gain commas. Do not alternate punctuation. If a dash is at the beginning of a statement, then do not put a parenthesis at the ending of the statement.

Tense

Items in a series will also have the same tense.
If past tense is being used for the other items in the series, then maintain the same past tense for your response.

Example: sailed, flew, and raced

If present participle tense is being used for the other items in the series, then maintain the same present participle tense for your response.

Example: sailing, flying, and racing

In order to test the tense of a verb, you can put it into a sentence that includes yourself. I sailed the boat. I flew the plane. I raced the car. These all fit into similar sentence structures and are in fact the same tense.

Added phrases

Any sentence or phrase added to a paragraph must maintain the same train of thought. This is particularly true when the word "and" is used. The word "and" joins two comments of like nature.

Example: These men were tough. They were accustomed to a hard life, and could watch a man die without blinking.

If an added phrase does not maintain a consistent train of thought, it will be set out with a word such as "but", "however", or "although". The new phrase would then be inconsistent to the train of thought and would offer a contrast.

Example: These men were tough. They were accustomed to a hard life, but to watch a man die would cause them to faint.

A tough man accustomed to a hard life is not expected to faint. Therefore the statements are contrasting and must have a contrasting transitional word, such as "but."

Word Confusion

Contractions

All contractions, such as they're, it's, and who's are actually two words joined together by the use of an apostrophe to replace a missing letter or letters. Whenever a contraction is encountered, it can be broken down into the two distinct words that make it up.

Example: I wouldn't eat in the cafeteria. = I would not eat in the cafeteria.

The apostrophe in the contraction is always located where the missing letter or letters should be. In the examples below, the apostrophe replaces the "o" in the word "not". The contraction "doesn't" actually stands for the two words "does not".

Incorrect Example: He does'nt live here.
Correct Example: He doesn't live here.

Whenever there is a contraction in an answer choice, it can always be replaced by the two words that make the contraction up. If necessary, scratch through the contractions in the choices, and replace them with the two words that make up the contraction. Otherwise the choices may be confusing. Alternatively, while reading the answer choices to yourself, instead of reading the contractions as a contraction, read them as the two separate words that make them up. Some contractions are especially confusing.

Its/It's
"It's" is actually a contraction for the two words "it is". Never confuse "it's" for the possessive pronoun "its". "It's" should only be used when the two words "it is" would make sense as a replacement. Use "its" in all other cases.

Example 1: It's going to rain later today. = It is going to rain later today.
Example 2: The dog chewed through its rope and ran away.

They're/Their/There
"They're" is actually a contraction for "they are", and those two words should always be used to replace "they're" when it is encountered.

Example: They're going to the movie with us. = They are going to the movie with us.

"Their" is an adjective used to show ownership.

Example 1: Their car is a red convertible.
Example 2: The students from each school sat in their own stands.

"There" should be used in all other cases.
Example 1: There exists an answer to every question.
Example 2: The man was over there.

Who's/Whose

Who's is actually a contraction for "who is", and those two words should always be used to replace who's when it is encountered.
Example: Who's going with me? = Who is going with me?

Whose would be used in all other cases, where "who is" does not fit.
Example: Whose car is this?

Their/His

"Their" is a plural possessive pronoun, referring to multiple people or objects.
Example: The men went to their cars.

"His" is a singular possessive, referring to an individual person or object.
Example: The man went to his car.

Which/That/Who

"Which" should be used to refer to things only.
John's dog, which was called Max, is large and fierce.

"That" may be used to refer to either persons or things.
Is this the only book that Louis L'Amour wrote?
Is Louis L'Amour the author that [or who] wrote Western novels?

"Who" should be used to refer to persons only.

Mozart was the composer who [or that] wrote those operas.

Who/Whom or Whoever/Whomever

Who/whom will be encountered in two forms, as an interrogative pronoun in a question, or as a relative pronoun not in a question.

1. Interrogative pronoun in a question. If the answer to the question would include the pronouns he, she, we, or they, then "who" is correct.

Example: Who threw the ball? He threw the ball.

If the answer to the question would include the pronouns him, her, us, or them, then "whom" is correct.
Example: With whom did you play baseball? I played baseball with him.

2. Relative pronoun NOT in a question.

If who/whom is followed by a verb, typically use "who".

Example: Peter Jackson was an obscure director who became a celebrity overnight.

If who/whom is followed by a noun, typically use "whom".

Example: Bob, whom we follow throughout his career, rose swiftly up the ladder of success.

However, beware of the insertion of phrases or expressions immediately following the use of who/whom. Sometimes, the phrase can be skipped without the sentence losing its meaning.
Example: This is the woman who, we believe, will win the race.

To determine the proper selection of who/whom, skip the phrase "we believe". Thus, "who" would come before "will win", a verb, making the choice of "who" correct.

In other cases, the sentence should be rephrased in order to make the right decision.

Example: I can't remember who the author of "War and Peace" is.
To determine the proper selection of who/whom, rephrase the sentence to state, "I can't remember who is the author of 'War and Peace'."

Correct pronoun usage in combinations
To determine the correct pronoun form in a compound subject, try each subject separately with the verb, adapting the form as necessary. Your ear will tell you which form is correct.

Example: Bob and (I, me) will be going.
Restate the sentence twice, using each subject individually. Bob will be going. I will be going.
"Me will be going" does not make sense.

When a pronoun is used with a noun immediately following (as in "we boys"), say the sentence without the added noun. Your ear will tell you the correct pronoun form.

Example: (We/Us) boys played football last year.
Restate the sentence twice, without the noun. We played football last year. Us played football last year. Clearly "We played football last year" makes more sense.

Commas

Flow

Commas break the flow of text. To test whether they are necessary, while reading the text to yourself, pause for a moment at each comma. If the pauses seem natural, then the commas are correct. If they are not, then the commas are not correct.

Nonessential clauses and phrases

A comma should be used to set off nonessential clauses and nonessential participial phrases from the rest of the sentence. To determine if a clause is essential, remove it from the sentence. If the removal of the clause would alter the meaning of the sentence, then it is essential. Otherwise, it is nonessential.

Example: John Smith, who was a disciple of Andrew Collins, was a noted archeologist.

In the example above, the sentence describes John Smith's fame in archeology. The fact that he was a disciple of Andrew Collins is not necessary to that meaning. Therefore, separating it from the rest of the sentence with commas, is correct.

Do not use a comma if the clause or phrase is essential to the meaning of the sentence.

Example: Anyone who appreciates obscure French poetry will enjoy reading the book.

If the phrase "who appreciates obscure French poetry" is removed, the sentence would indicate that anyone would enjoy reading the book, not just those with an appreciation for obscure French poetry. However, the sentence implies that the book's enjoyment may not be for everyone, so the phrase is essential.

Another perhaps easier way to determine if the clause is essential is to see if it has a comma at its beginning or end. Consistent, parallel punctuation must be used, and so if you can determine a comma exists at one side of the clause, then you can be certain that a comma should exist on the opposite side.

Subjects and verbs

Subjects and verbs must not be separated by commas. However, a pair of commas setting off a nonessential phrase is allowed.

Example: The office, which closed today for the festival, was open on Thursday.
"Was" is the verb, while "office" is the subject. The comma pair between them sets off a nonessential phrase, "which is allowed". A single comma between them would not be allowed.

If you are trying to find the subject, first find the verb and use it to fill in the blank in the following sentence. Who or what ___?

Example: The boy on the bicycle raced down the hill.
The verb is "raced". If you can find "raced" and identify it as the verb, ask yourself, "Who or what raced down the hill?" The answer to that question is the subject, in this case "boy".

Independent clauses

Use a comma before the words and, but, or, nor, for, yet when they join independent clauses. To determine if two clauses are independent, remove the word that joins them. If the two clauses are capable of being their own sentence by themselves, then they are independent and need a comma between them.

Example: He ran down the street, and then he ran over the bridge.
He ran down the street. Then he ran over the bridge. These are both clauses capable of being their own sentence. Therefore a comma must be used along with the word "and" to join the two clauses together.

If one or more of the clauses would be a fragment if left alone, then it must be joined to another clause and does not need a comma between them.

Example: He ran down the street and over the bridge.
He ran down the street. Over the bridge. "Over the bridge" is a sentence fragment and is not capable of existing on its own. No comma is necessary to join it with "He ran down the street".

Note that this does not cover the use of "and" when separating items in a series, such as "red, white, and blue". In these cases a comma is not always necessary between the last two items in the series, but in general it is best to use one.

Parenthetical expressions

Commas should separate parenthetical expressions such as the following: after all, by the way, for example, in fact, on the other hand.
Example: By the way, she is in my biology class.

If the parenthetical expression is in the middle of the sentence, a comma would be both before and after it.
Example: She is, after all, in my biology class.

However, these expressions are not always used parenthetically. In these cases, commas are not used. To determine if an expression is parenthetical, see if it would need a pause if you were reading the text. If it does, then it is parenthetical and needs commas.

Example: You can tell by the way she plays the violin that she enjoys its music.
No pause is necessary in reading that example sentence. Therefore the phrase "by the way" does not need commas around it.

Sentence beginnings

Use a comma after words such as so, well, yes, no, and why when they begin a sentence.

Example 1: So, you were there when they visited.

Example 2: Well, I really haven't thought about it.

Example 3: Yes, I heard your question.

Example 4: No, I don't think I'll go to the movie.

Example 5: Why, I can't imagine where I left my keys.

Hyphens

Hyphenate a compound adjective that is directly before the noun it describes.

Example 1: He was the best-known kid in the school.

Example 2: The shot came from that grass-covered hill.

Example 3: The well-drained fields were dry soon after the rain.

Semicolons

Period replacement

A semicolon is often described as either a weak period or strong comma. Semicolons should separate independent clauses that could stand alone as separate sentences. To test where a semicolon should go, replace it with a period in your mind. If the two independent clauses would seem normal with the period, then the semicolon is in the right place.

Example: The rain had finally stopped; a few rays of sunshine were pushing their way through the clouds.

The rain had finally stopped. A few rays of sunshine were pushing their way through the clouds. These two sentences can exist independently with a period between them. Because they are also closely related in thought, a semicolon is a good choice to combine them.

Related/Unrelated

A semicolon should only join clauses that are closely related in thought.
Example: The lasagna is delicious; I'll have another piece.
In this example, the two clauses are closely related in thought; a semicolon should join them.

Do not use a semicolon if the clauses are unrelated in thought.

Example: For Steve, oil painting was a difficult medium to master. He had enjoyed taking photographs when he was younger.
In this example, the two sentences would be unrelated clauses, so a semicolon should not join them.

Comparative methods of joining clauses

Use a semicolon between independent clauses not joined by "and, but, for, or, nor, yet, so, since, therefore". Semicolons should rarely be next to these words, but is rather used in place of a comma and these words.

Example 1: He had the gun; it hung from a holster at his side.
In the example above, no "and" or comma is necessary.

Example 2: He had the gun, and it hung from a holster at his side.
In the example above, the comma combined with the word "and" help to join the two independent clauses.

Transitions

When a semicolon is next to a transition word, such as "however", it comes before the word.

Example: The man in the red shirt stood next to her; however, he did not know her name.

If these two clauses were separated with a period, the period would go before the word "however" creating the following two sentences: The man in the red shirt stood next to her. However, he did not know her name. The semicolon can function as a weak period and join the two clauses by replacing the period.

Items in a series

Semicolons are used to separate 3 or more items in a series that have a comma internally.

Example: The club president appointed the following to chair the various committees: John Smith, planning; Jessica Graham, membership; Paul Randolph, financial; and Jerry Short, legal.

Parentheses

Years

Parentheses should be used around years.

Example: The presidency of Franklin Delano Roosevelt (1932-1945) was the longest one in American history.

Nonessential information

Parentheses can be used around information that is added to a sentence but is not essential. Commas or dashes could also be used around these nonessential phrases.

Example: George Eliot (whose real name was Mary Ann Evans) wrote poems and several well-known novels.

Colon

Items in a series

A colon should precede a list of items in which you could logically insert the word "namely" after it.

Example: The syllabus stated that each student would need the following: a sketch pad, a set of paint brushes, an easel, a pencil, and a box of crayons.

If the word namely were inserted, the example sentence would read, "The syllabus stated that each student would need the following: "namely" a sketch pad, a set of paint brushes, an easel, a pencil, and a box of crayons." Because the sentence still flows with the word "namely" inserted, a colon is necessary.

When the list immediately follows a verb or preposition, do not use a colon.

Example 1: The emergency kit included safety flares, jumper cables, and a flashlight.
Example 2: Each student taking the test was provided with two sharpened pencils, paper, a calculator, and a ruler.
Note that the insertion of the word "namely" would be awkward in the above two examples.

Independent clauses

Use a colon between independent clauses when the second clause explains or restates the idea of the first.

Example: Benjamin Franklin had many talents: he was an inventor, a writer, a politician, and a philosopher.

Apostrophes

If the noun is plural and ends in an "s", the possessive apostrophe would come after the word, without the addition of another "s".

Example: The students' hats were wet from the rain.

In the example above, there are plural or many students, all of whom have wet hats.

If the noun is plural and does not end in an "s", the possessive apostrophe would come after the word, with the addition of an "s".

Example: The mice's feet were wet from the rain.

If the noun is singular, the possessive apostrophe is followed by an "s".

Example: The student's hat was wet from the rain.

In the example above, there is only one student, whose hat is wet.

Use Your Ear

Read each sentence carefully, inserting the answer choices in the blanks. Don't stop at the first answer choice if you think it is right, but read them all. What may seem like the best choice, at first, may not be after you have had time to read all of the choices. Allow your ear to determine what sounds right. Often one or two answer choices can be immediately ruled out because it doesn't make sound logical or make sense.

Contextual Clues

It bears repeating that contextual clues offer a lot of help in determining the best answer. Key words in the sentence will allow you to determine exactly which answer choice is the best replacement text.

Example:

Archeology has shown that some of the ruins of the ancient city of Babylon are approximately 500 years <u>as old as any supposed</u> Mesopotamian predecessors.

A.) as old as their supposed

B.) older than their supposed

In this example, the key word "supposed" is used. Archaeology would either confirm that the predecessors to Babylon were more ancient or disprove that supposition. Since supposed was used, it would imply that archaeology had disproved the accepted belief, making Babylon actually older, not as old as, and answer choice "B" correct.

Furthermore, because "500 years" is used, answer choice A can be ruled out. Years are used to show either absolute or relative age. If two objects are as old as each other, no years are necessary to describe that relationship, and it would be sufficient to say, "The ancient city of Babylon is approximately as old as their supposed Mesopotamian predecessors," without using the term "500 years".

The Writing Essay Test

The CAAP Writing Essay Test is predicated on the assumption that the skills most commonly taught in college-level writing courses and required in upper-division college courses across the curriculum include:

- Formulating an assertion about a given issue
- Supporting that assertion with evidence appropriate to the issue, position taken, and a given audience
- Organizing and connecting major ideas
- Expressing those ideas in clear, effective language

The model developed by CAAP for the Writing Essay Test is designed to elicit responses that demonstrate a student's ability to perform these skills. Two 20-minute writing tasks are defined by a short prompt that identifies a specific hypothetical situation and audience. The hypothetical situation involves an issue on which the examinee must take a stand. An examinee is instructed to take a position on the issue and to explain to the audience why the position taken is the better (or best) alternative.

In order to more clearly define the audience and provide a focus for responses, each prompt specifies the basis upon which the audience will make its decision. Situations and audiences defined in the writing prompts are constructed so that the required background knowledge and experience are within the command of college sophomores.

For the CAAP Writing Essay Test, ACT developed a six-point, modified holistic scoring system. Each essay is read by two trained raters who independently score the essay on a scale from 1 to 6 (1 being the lowest score, 6 the highest). The scores from the two raters for each of the two essays (four scores) are averaged for the reported score, which ranges from 1 to 6 in increments of .5. The two raters' scores for each essay must either agree or be adjacent to be averaged. If the raters' scores differ by two or more points, a chief scorer adjudicates and determines the reported score.

Each score point reflects a student's ability to perform the skills identified above. Essays are evaluated according to how well a student formulates a clear assertion on the issue defined in the prompt, supports that assertion with reasons and evidence appropriate to the position taken and the specified concerns of the audience, and develops the argument in a coherent and logical manner. A student obtains lower scores for not taking a position on the specified issue, for not developing the argument, or for not expressing those ideas in clear, effective language. A student who does not respond to the prompt is assigned a "not rateable" indicator rather than a score on the 1 to 6 scale.

Brainstorm

Spend the first three to five minutes brainstorming out ideas. Write down any ideas you might have on the topic. The purpose is to extract from the recesses of your memory any relevant information. In this stage, anything goes down. Write down any idea, regardless of how good it may initially seem. You can use either the scratch paper provided or the word processor to quickly jot down your thoughts and ideas. The word processor is highly recommended though, particularly if you are a fast typist.

Strength through Diversity

The best papers will contain diversity of examples and reasoning. As you brainstorm consider different perspectives. Not only are there two sides to every issue, but there are also countless perspectives that can be considered. On any issue, different groups are impacted, with many reaching the same conclusion or position, but through vastly different paths. Try to "see" the issue through as many different eyes as you can. Look at it from every angle and from every vantage point. The more diverse the reasoning used, the more balanced the paper will become and the better the score.

Example:

The issue of free trade is not just two sided. It impacts politicians, domestic (US) manufacturers, foreign manufacturers, the US economy, the world economy, strategic alliances, retailers, wholesalers, consumers, unions, workers, and the exchange of more than just goods, but also of ideas, beliefs, and cultures. The more of these angles that you can approach the issue from, the more solid your reasoning and the stronger your position.

Furthermore, don't just use information as to how the issue impacts other people. Draw liberally from your own experience and your own observations. Explain a personal experience that you have had and your own emotions from that moment. Anything that you've seen in your community or observed in society can be expanded upon to further round out your position on the issue.

Pick a Main Idea

Once you have finished with your creative flow, stop and review it. Which idea were you able to come up with the most supporting information? It's extremely important that you pick an angle that will allow you to have a thorough and comprehensive coverage of the topic. This is not about your personal convictions, but about writing a concise rational discussion of an idea.

Weed the Garden

Every garden of ideas gets weeds in it. The ideas that you brainstormed over are going to be random pieces of information of mixed value. Go through it methodically and pick out the ones that are the best. The best ideas are strong points that it will be easy to write a few sentences or a paragraph about.

Create a Logical Flow

Now that you know which ideas you are going to use and focus upon, organize them. Put your writing points in a logical order. You have your main ideas that you will focus on, and must align them in a sequence that will flow in a smooth, sensible path from point to point, so that the reader will go smoothly from one idea to the next in a logical path. Readers must have a sense of continuity as they read your paper. You don't want to have a paper that rambles back and forth.

Start Your Engines

You have a logical flow of main ideas with which to start writing. Begin expanding on the issues in the sequence that you have set for yourself. Pace yourself. Don't spend too much time on any one of the ideas that you are expanding upon. You want to have time for all of them. Make sure you watch your time. If you have ten minutes left to write out your ideas and you have ten ideas, then you can only use one minute per idea. It can be a daunting task to cram a lot of information down in words in a short amount of time, but if you pace yourself, you can get through it all. If you find that you are falling behind, speed up. Move through each idea more quickly, spending less time to expand upon the idea in order to catch back up.

Once you finish expanding on each idea, go back to your brainstorming session up above, where you wrote out your ideas. Go ahead and erase the ideas as you write about them. This will let you see what you need to write about next, and also allow you to pace yourself and see what you have left to cover.

First Paragraph

Your first paragraph should have several easily identifiable features.

First, it should have a quick description or paraphrasing of the topic. Use your own words to briefly explain what the topic is about.

Second, you should explain your opinion of the topic and give an explanation of why you feel that way. What is your decision or conclusion on the topic?

Third, you should list your "writing points". What are the main ideas that you came up with earlier? This is your opportunity to outline the rest of your paper. Have a sentence explaining each idea that you will go intend further depth in additional paragraphs. If someone was to only read this paragraph, they should be able to get an "executive summary" of the entire paper.

Body Paragraph

Each of your successive paragraphs should expand upon one of the points listed in the main paragraph. Use your personal experience and knowledge to support each of your points. Examples should back up everything.

Conclusion Paragraph

Once you have finished expanding upon each of your main points, wrap it up. Summarize what you have said and covered in a conclusion paragraph. Explain once more your opinion of the topic and quickly review why you feel that way. At this stage, you have already backed up your statements, so there is no need to do that again. All you are doing is refreshing in the mind of the reader the main points that you have made.

Don't Panic

Panicking will not put down any more words on paper for you. Therefore, it isn't helpful. When you first see the topic, if your mind goes as blank as the page on which you have to write out your paper, take a deep breath. Force yourself to mechanically go through the steps listed above.

Secondly, don't get clock fever. It's easy to be overwhelmed when you're looking at a page that doesn't seem to have much text, there is a lot of blank space further down, your mind is full of random thoughts and feeling confused, and the clock is ticking down faster than you would like. You brainstormed first so that you don't have to keep coming up with ideas. If you're running out of time and you have a lot of ideas that you haven't expanded upon, don't be afraid to make some cuts. Start picking the best ideas that you have left and expand on those few. Don't feel like you have to write down and expand all of your ideas.

Check Your Work

It is more important to have a shorter paper that is well written and well organized, than a longer paper that is poorly written and poorly organized. Don't keep writing about a subject just to add words and sentences, and certainly don't start repeating yourself. Expand on the ideas that you identified in the brainstorming session and make sure that you save yourself a few minutes at the end to go back and check your work.

Leave time at the end, at least three minutes, to go back and check over your work. Reread and make sure that everything you've written makes sense and flows. Clean up any spelling or grammar mistakes that you might have made. If you see anything that needs to be moved around, such as a paragraph that would fit in better somewhere else, cut and paste it to that new location. Also, go ahead and erase any brainstorming ideas that you weren't able to expand upon and clean up any other extraneous information that you might have written that doesn't fit into your paper.

As you proofread, make sure there aren't any fragments or run-ons. Check for sentences that are too short or too long. If the sentence is too short, look to see if you have an identifiable subject and verb. If it is too long, break it up into two separate sentences. Watch out for any "big" words you may have used. It's good to use difficult vocabulary words, but only if you are positive that you are using them correctly. Your paper has to be correct, it doesn't have to be fancy. You're not trying to impress anyone with your vocabulary, just your ability to develop and express ideas.

Final Note

Depending on your test taking preferences and personality, the essay writing will probably be your hardest or your easiest section. You are required to go through the entire process of writing a paper in 20 minutes or less, which can be quite a challenge.

Focus upon each of the steps listed above. Go through the process of creative flow first, generating ideas and thoughts about the topic. Then organize those ideas into a smooth logical flow. Pick out the ones that are best from the list you have created. Decide which main idea or angle of the topic you will discuss.

Create a recognizable structure in your paper, with an introductory paragraph explaining what you have decided upon, and what your main points will be. Use the body paragraphs to expand on those main points and have a conclusion that wraps up the issue or topic.

Save a few moments to go back and review what you have written. Clean up any minor mistakes that you might have had and give it those last few critical touches that can make a huge difference. Finally, be proud and confident of what you have written!

The Science Test

The CAAP Science Test is a 45-item, 40-minute test designed to measure students' skills in scientific reasoning. The contents of the Science Test are drawn from biological sciences (e.g., biology, botany, and zoology), chemistry, physics, and the physical sciences (e.g., geology, astronomy, and meteorology). The test emphasizes scientific reasoning skills rather than recall of scientific content or a high level of skill in mathematics or reading. A total score is provided for the Science Test; no subscores are provided.

The test consists of eight passage sets, each of which contains scientific information and a set of multiple-choice test questions. A passage may conform to one of the three different formats listed below.

- Data Representation. This format presents students with graphic and tabular material similar to that found in science journals and texts. The items associated with this format measure skills such as graph reading, interpretation of scatterplots, and interpretation of information presented in tables, diagrams, and figures.

- Research Summaries. This format provides students with descriptions of one experiment or of several related experiments. The items focus on the design of experiments and the interpretation of experimental results. The stimulus and items are written expressly for the Science Test, and all relevant information is completely presented in the text of the stimulus or in the test questions.

- Conflicting Viewpoints. This format presents students with several hypotheses or views that are mutually inconsistent owing to differing premises, incomplete or disputed data, or differing interpretations of data. The stimuli may include illustrative charts, graphs, tables, diagrams, or figures. Items in this format measure students' skills in understanding, analyzing, and comparing alternative viewpoints or hypotheses.

The 45 test items in the Science Test can be conceptualized in three major groups. Each group is meant to address an important major element of scientific inquiry. The groups are listed below, along with brief descriptions of typical knowledge and skills tested.

- Understanding. Identify and evaluate scientific concepts, assumptions, and components of an experimental design or process; identify and evaluate data presented in graphs, figures, or tables; translate given data into an alternate form.

- Analyzing. Process information needed to draw conclusions or to formulate hypotheses; determine whether information provided supports a given hypothesis or conclusion; evaluate, compare, and contrast experimental designs or viewpoints; specify alternative ways of testing hypotheses or viewpoints.

- Generalizing. Extend information given to a broader or different context; generate a model consistent with given information; develop new procedures to gain new information; use given information to predict outcomes.

The Science test will scare you. For even the most accomplished student, most of the terms will be unfamiliar. General test-taking skill will help the most. DO NOT run out of time, move quickly, and use the easy pacing methods we outlined in the test-taking tactics section.

The most important thing you can do is to ignore your fears and jump into the test immediately- do not be overwhelmed by all of the strange-sounding terms. You have to jump into the test like jumping into a pool- all at once is the easiest way. Once you get past the jargon, you'll find that the Science test is easier than even the Reading Test- at least you can be sure of answer- but most students never finish the

Science test. This is why managing your time on this test is at least as important as on the math test.

The first thing to do is to read the passage. Use 2 minutes to do this- really try to understand what's going on, treating all of the scientific terms as you would characters in a novel- just accept their names as they are, and follow the story. Use another 3 minutes to answer as many questions as you can; then, MOVE ON to the next section. It's important to answer all of the easy questions.

Overall, the science is the test that is hardest to study for, and surprisingly, has the lowest test average for all test-takers, even lower than the Math. If Science is a subject you take because you have to, and not because you want to, your primary goal on Science is damage control- keep it from dragging down your higher scores when CAAP averages your test scores to get the composite.

The Science test is also unlike any other science test you've probably ever taken in high school. It's vital that you work a few practice Science tests before the test day- that alone will boost your score if you've never taken the CAAP before.

Three Types of Passages

1. Graph and Table Mania- 2 or more tables or graphs with questions about their meaning. You should start by asking yourself basic questions including: What are the variables? What are the units of measure?, What are the values of the variables?, What are the trends?, and What are the correlations?.
2. Fighting Scientists- 2 different theories are explained for a natural process, you answer questions about them. Short paragraphs will be provided representing the ideas of two scientists. They will disagree with each other. Your job is to analyze that argument and information in the two paragraphs. Approach it with the

following questions. What is the nature of the disagreement? How has the opinion been reached? What forms of evidence might resolve the conflict? What are the points of agreement and disagreement? What evidence supports or denies support for either viewpoint?

3. Experiments- questions about data from experiments (usually 2) performed. Experiment descriptions will be provided, along with a statement of the experiment's results. You should start by asking yourself basic questions including: What is the experiment designed to find out?, What does the experimental method or any accompanying diagrams reveal? What are the variables? What are the controls? (Controls are precautions taken to eliminate all variables except the independent variable.) What are the results? Look for flaws in the experiment. Are the controls adequate? Is the conclusion justified by the data? Are the experimental errors so great as to invalidate the results? Once you thoroughly understand the nature of the experiment and the meaning of the results, you should be able to deal with the multiple-choice questions based on the experiment.

Four Types of Questions

1. Fact- this question asks for a fact, usually some sort of number, based on the passage. For example, "what is the volume of the gas at 1 atmosphere?" followed by choices.

2. Graphs- This type asks you to pick between graphs that best represent something described in the question.

3. Short answer- a short answer, either a word or phrase, that answers a question about the passage. This question is spotted not by the length of the answers (though they are usually short), but by how much "thought" is in the answer choice. For example, choices that read "Day 1 at 12:00 PM, Day 2 at 4:00 PM," etc., would be short answer even though they are long. The question is still looking for a simple fact.

4. Long answer- an interpretation question from the passage that requires you to decide between several possible extended answers.

There are three question difficulty levels- Understanding, analysis, and generalization. In each group of questions, the first ones will be understanding, then will come the analysis questions, and finally the generalization questions. These are in increasing levels of difficulty as the earlier questions ask easy to find answers, while the later questions involve greater depth of interpretation and the ability to draw conclusions from the data.

Answer Choice Elimination Techniques

Slang

Scientific sounding answers are better than slang ones. In the answer choices below, choice B is much less scientific and is incorrect, while choice A is a scientific analytical choice and is correct.

Example:

A.) To compare the outcomes of the two different kinds of treatment.

B.) Because some subjects insisted on getting one or the other of the treatments.

Extreme Statements

Avoid wild answers that throw out highly controversial ideas that are proclaimed as established fact. Choice A is a radical idea and is incorrect. Choice B is a calm rational statement. Notice that Choice B does not make a definitive, uncompromising stance, using a hedge word "if" to provide wiggle room.

Example:

A.) Bypass surgery should be discontinued completely.

B.) Medication should be used instead of surgery for patients who have not had a heart attack if they suffer from mild chest pain and mild coronary artery blockage.

Similar Answer Choices

When you have two answer choices that are direct opposites, one of them is usually the correct answer.

Example:

A.) The effectiveness of enzyme I at 30 degrees Celsius depends on its concentration.
B.) The effectiveness of enzyme II at 30 degrees Celsius depends on its concentration.

These two answer choices are very similar and fall into the same family of answer choices. A family of answer choices is when two or three answer choices are very similar. Often two will be opposites and one may show an equality.

Example:
A.) Operation I or Operation II can be conducted at equal cost
B.) Operation I would be less expensive than Operation II
C.) Operation II would be less expensive than Operation I
D.) Neither Operation I nor Operation II would be effective at preventing the spread of cancer.
E.) Both Operations would be effective

Note how the first three choices are all related. They all ask about a cost comparison. Beware of immediately recognizing choices B and C as opposites and choosing one of those two. Choice A is in the same family of questions and should be considered as well. However, choice D and E is not in the same family of questions. It has nothing to do with cost and can be discounted in most cases.

Related to the family of answers concept are answer choices that have similar parts. Example:

A.) The first stage of reaction 1 and the first stage of reaction 2.

B.) The second stage of reaction 1 and the second stage of reaction 3.

C.) The second stage of reaction 1 and the second stage of reaction 2.

D.) The second stage of reaction 1 and the first stage of reaction 2.

In this question, answer choices B, C, and D all begin with the same phrase "the second stage of reaction 1". This means answer choice A can be eliminated. Then answer choices A and D both have the same phrase "the first stage of reaction 2". Also, answer choices B and C have different phrases. This means that either A or D is the correct answer. Since choice A has already been eliminated, D is probably the right answer. In these cases similar phrases identify answer choices as being members of the same family of answers. Each answer choice that has a similar phrase is in the same family of answers. Answer choices that fall into the most family of answers is usually the correct answer.

Once again, hedge words are usually good, while answer choices without hedge words are typically wrong. Answer choices that say "exactly", "always" are often wrong.

Hedging

When asked for a conclusion that may be drawn, look for critical "hedge" phrases, such as likely, may, can, will often, sometimes, etc, often, almost, mostly, usually, generally, rarely, sometimes. Question writers insert these hedge phrases to cover every possibility. Often an answer will be wrong simply because it leaves no room for exception. Avoid answer choices that have definitive words like "exactly," and "always".

Time Management

Scan the passage to get a rough idea of what it is asking.

Avoid answers that while they are obviously true they don't answer the question. Answers must ANSWER the question, not just be factually true statements. The answer choice must be based strictly on the contents of the passage and question.

Read all the choices. Later answer choices will often bring up a new point that you may not have considered. As you read the choices, scratch through the ones that you know are wrong, but don't make your final selection until you read them all.

The easier "understanding" questions are listed first. Do not skip these first questions in each group, though everywhere else (on other tests and in other questions in the science test that aren't the first question in a group) skip questions giving you too much difficulty. This is because if you don't understand the passage, you're in trouble on the latter questions. Make sure you know enough to get the first question right, because the other questions will all flow from a basic understanding of the passage.

Skip the hard questions that aren't the first question in a group.

Estimation

For some numerical questions, estimate. Calculation takes time, and you should avoid it whenever possible. You can usually eliminate three obviously wrong choices quite easily. For example, suppose a graph shows that an object has traveled 48 meters in 11 seconds, and you are asked to find its speed. You are given these choices:

A. 250 m/s
B. 42 m/s

C. 4.4 m/s

D. 1.2 m/s

E. 0.5 m/s

You know that 48 divided by 11 will be a little over 4, so you can pick out C as the answer without ever doing the calculation.

Highly Technical Questions May Not Be

Sometimes a single piece of information may be given to you. For example, blood velocity is lowest in the capillaries (averaging 3cm/sec).

A question may ask the following:

A physician examining a newly discovered tribe of people deep in the Amazon jungles found that the relative total surface area of their capillaries was greater than that previously reported for any other people. If the physician were to predict the average velocity of blood through their capillaries, which of the following values would be the most reasonable.

A.) 2 cm/sec

B.) 3 cm/sec

C.) 4 cm/sec

D.) 5 cm/sec

You know that 3 cm/sec is the standard, which is choice B. Without understanding any of the subject matter or even reading the associated graph, it is possible to choose the correct answer, which is A. The reason is because there is only answer, which is less than 3 cm/sec, while there are two answers that are greater than 3 cm/sec. Since you are not looking for an exact answer, but only a reasonable answer, then you can conclude that if the correct answer was greater than 3 cm/sec, TWO answer choices would meet that criteria. However, if the correct answer is less than 3 cm/sec, only ONE answer choice meets that criteria, meaning it is likely the correct answer.

Experiment Passages

The best way to remember three different but similar experiments is to focus on the differences between the experiments. Between the first and second experiment, what was changed? Between the second and third experiment, what was done differently? That will keep the overall experiments properly aligned in your mind. What variables changed between the experiments?

Random Tips

- On fact questions that require choosing between numbers, don't guess the smallest or largest choice unless you're sure of the answer (remember- "sure" means you would bet $5 on it).
- Short answer questions want you to choose between several words that are choices. Your best weapon on these is process of elimination- there are no easy tips.
- The long answer questions will often have a few "bizarre" choices, mentioning things that are not relevant to the passage. Also avoid answers that sound "smart." Again, if you're willing to bet $5, disregard the tips and go with your bet.
- In passages that describe a series of experiments, often the questions will ask you if the researcher made a mistake, or could improve the experiments by making some change; the answer choices will be two yes's and two no's, each

with a different justification. Usually, the answer is one of the "no" choices- CAAP does not include deliberately flawed experiments in passages, so it is safe to assume that whatever suggestion the question poses would NOT improve the experiment. Of course, if you KNOW ($5 confidence) otherwise, disregard the tip.

- This bears repeating, especially on this test: you have probably never had a science test quite like the CAAP Science. More than any other test, you MUST take at least one practice test so as to not be bogged down with the unfamiliar format.

The Critical Thinking Test

The CAAP Critical Thinking Test is a 32-item, 40-minute test that measures students' skills in clarifying, analyzing, evaluating, and extending arguments. An argument is defined as a sequence of statements that includes a claim that one of the statements, the conclusion, follows from the other statements. The Critical Thinking Test consists of four passages that are representative of the kinds of issues commonly encountered in a postsecondary curriculum.

A passage typically presents a series of subarguments in support of a more general conclusion or conclusions. Each passage presents one or more arguments using a variety of formats, including case studies, debates, dialogues, overlapping positions, statistical arguments, experimental results, or editorials. Each passage is accompanied by a set of multiple-choice test items. A total score is provided for the Critical Thinking Test; no subcores are provided.

Milk the Passage
Some of the passages may throw you completely off. They might deal with a subject you have not been exposed to, or one that you haven't reviewed in years. While your lack of knowledge about the subject will be a hindrance, the passage itself can give you many clues that will help you find the correct answer. Read the passage carefully, and look for clues. Watch particularly for adjectives and nouns describing difficult terms or words that you don't recognize. Regardless of if you understand a word or not, replacing it with the synonyms used for it in the passage may help you to understand what the questions are asking.
Example: A bacteriophage is a virus that infects bacteria....

While you may not know much about the characteristics of a bacteriophage, the fifth word into the passage told you that a bacteriophage is a virus. Wherever you see the word "bacteriophage," you can mentally replace it with the word "virus". Your more general knowledge of viruses may enable you to answer the question.

Look carefully for these descriptive synonyms (nouns) and adjectives and use them to help you understand the difficult terms. Rather than wracking your mind about specific detail information concerning a difficult term in the passage, use the more general description or synonym provided to make it easier for you.

Make Predictions

One convenience of questions with short paragraphs full of information is that you can easily remember the few facts presented, compared to a much longer passage full of much more information. As you read and understand the passage and then the question, try to guess what the answer will be. Remember that four of the five answer choices are wrong, and once you begin reading them, your mind will immediately become cluttered with answer choices designed to throw you off. Your mind is typically the most focused immediately after you have read the passage and question and digested its contents. If you can, try to predict what the correct answer will be. You may be surprised at what you can predict.

Quickly scan the choices and see if your prediction is in the listed answer choices. If it is, then you can be quite confident that you have the right answer. It still won't hurt to check the other answer choices, but most of the time, you've got it!

Benchmark

After you read the first answer choice, decide if you think it sounds correct or not. If it doesn't, move on to the next answer choice. If it does, tentatively mark in your answer book beside that choice. This doesn't mean that you've definitely selected it as your answer choice; it just means that it's the best you've seen thus far. Go ahead and read the next choice. If the next choice is worse than the one you've already selected, keep going to the next answer choice. If the next choice is better than the choice you've already selected, mark the new answer choice as your best guess.

The first answer choice that you select becomes your standard. Every other answer choice must be benchmarked against that standard. That choice is correct until proven otherwise by another answer choice beating it out. Once you've decided that no other answer choice seems as good, do one final check to ensure that it answers the question posed.

New Information

Correct answers will usually contain the information listed in the paragraph and question. Rarely will completely new information be inserted into a correct answer choice. Occasionally the new information may be related in a manner than CAAP is asking for you to interpret, but seldom.

Example:

The argument above is dependent upon which of the following assumptions?

A. Scientists have used Charles's Law to interpret the relationship.

If Charles's Law is not mentioned at all in the referenced paragraph and argument, then it is unlikely that this choice is correct. All of the information needed to answer the question is provided for you, and so you should not have to make guesses that are unsupported or choose answer choices that have unknown information that cannot be reasoned.

Key Words

Look for answer choices that have the same key words in them as the question.

Example:

Which of the following, if true, would best explain the reluctance of politicians since 1980 to support this funding?

Look for the key words "since 1980" to be referenced in the correct answer choice. Most valid answer choices would probably include a phrase such as "since 1980, politicians have..."

Valid Information

Don't discount any of the information provided in short paragraphs. They are short to begin with and every piece of information may be necessary to determine the correct answer. None of the information in the paragraph is there to throw you off (while the answer choices will certainly have information to throw you off). If two seemingly unrelated topics are discussed, don't ignore either. You can be confident there is a relationship, or it wouldn't be included in the paragraph, and you are probably going to have to determine what is that relationship for the answer. The information may be broken into two sections, for example, there might be the term "situation" followed by a description, then the term "analysis" followed by a description. You will need both of these pieces of information to completely understand which answer choice is correct.

Don't Fall for the Obvious

When in doubt of the answer, it is easy to go with what you are familiar with. If you are familiar with one of the answer choices and know it is correct, then you may be inclined to guess at that term. Be careful though, and don't go with familiar answers simply because they are familiar.

Example: Which one of the following, if true, contributes most to an explanation of the result of changing the temperature of the solution to 212º F:

    A) The solution would immediately begin to boil.

    B) The increase in temperature would result in higher levels of concentrate needing to be added to maintain equilibrium.

    C) The reaction would become stabilized.

    D) Changing the temperature would saturate the solution.

    E) At 212º F the reaction would be more easily controlled.

You know that 212º F is the boiling point of pure water. Therefore choice A is familiar, because there is a link between the temperature 212º F and the word "boiling". If you are unsure of the correct answer, you may decide upon choice A simply because of its familiarity. Don't be deceived though. Think through the other answer choices before making your final selection. Just because you have a mental link between the question and an answer choice, doesn't make that answer choice correct.

Weird Answers

Don't be afraid to choose an answer choice that sounds weird. This is a test of your logical reasoning and weird answers can be perfectly logical given the right situation. Make sure that the answer choice you choose answers the question, regardless of how unusual it may seem. "All clocks have two hands" may not seem like a normal phrase to expect in a CAAP answer, but it still may be the right answer. Don't discount it until you've fully considered the answer choice as it relates to the question and situation posed.

Breakdown

When trying to identify the logical flaws in a statement, break it down into its components. Many statement may have more than one logical flaw or fallacy. Break the statement into the claims that it is making and analyze each one. Understand each individual relationship, so that you can compare those relationships to your answer choices. Don't fall for the surface similarities.

Example: All leaders have charisma. I am very charismatic. So I must be a great leader.

Which one of the following exhibits both of the logical flaws exhibited in the argument above?

A) All librarians have glasses. This person has glasses. So this person must be a librarian.

On the surface, this answer choice sounds correct. In fact, the statements even line up perfectly. All leaders have charisma ~ All librarians have glasses.

The problem is that this answer choice does not have BOTH logical flaws that were in the original statement. One of the two logical flaws dealt with intensification. I am VERY charismatic. So I must be a GREAT leader. Note how the rule of "if it's true for a little, then it must be true of a lot" was applied. Answer choice A does not have this intensification relationship.

Additionally, if asked for an answer choice which has the same logical flaws as a given statement, you can generally exclude one that is phrased exactly the same way. If the original statement says, "This group1 has this," then you can generally eliminate any answer choices that start with "This group2 has this." It's too obvious and is a trap!

Random Tips
- For questions that you're not clear on the answer, use the process of elimination. Weed out the answer choices that you know are wrong before choosing an answer.
- Don't fall for "bizarre" choices, mentioning things that are not relevant to the passage. Also avoid answers that sound "smart." Again, if you're willing to bet $5, ignore the tips and go with your bet.

Appendix A: Area, Volume, Surface Area Formulas

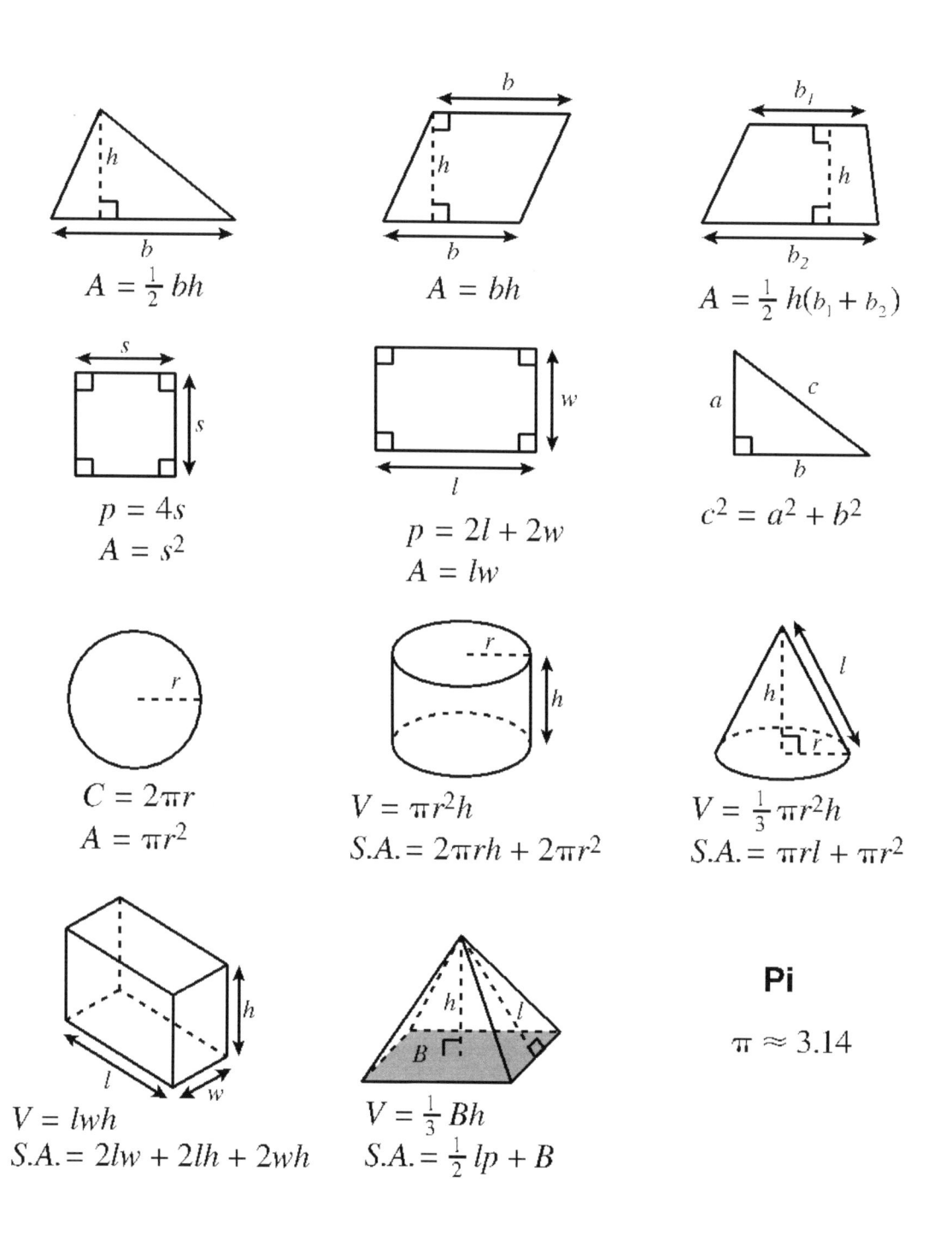

$A = \frac{1}{2}bh$

$A = bh$

$A = \frac{1}{2}h(b_1 + b_2)$

$p = 4s$
$A = s^2$

$p = 2l + 2w$
$A = lw$

$c^2 = a^2 + b^2$

$C = 2\pi r$
$A = \pi r^2$

$V = \pi r^2 h$
$S.A. = 2\pi rh + 2\pi r^2$

$V = \frac{1}{3}\pi r^2 h$
$S.A. = \pi rl + \pi r^2$

$V = lwh$
$S.A. = 2lw + 2lh + 2wh$

$V = \frac{1}{3}Bh$
$S.A. = \frac{1}{2}lp + B$

Pi

$\pi \approx 3.14$

Special Report: CAAP Secrets in Action

Sample Question from the Reading Test:

Mark Twain was well aware of his celebrity. He was among the first authors to employ a clipping service to track press coverage of himself, and it was not unusual for him to issue his own press statements if he wanted to influence or "spin" coverage of a particular story. The celebrity Twain achieved during his last ten years still reverberates today. Nearly all of his most popular novels were published before 1890, long before his hair grayed or he began to wear his famous white suit in public. We appreciate the author but seem to remember the celebrity.

Based on the passage above, Mark Twain seemed interested in:

A. maintaining his celebrity
B. selling more of his books
C. hiding his private life
D. gaining popularity

Let's look at a couple of different methods of solving this problem.

1. Identify the key words in each answer choice. These are the nouns and verbs that are the most important words in the answer choice.

A. maintaining, celebrity
B. selling, books

C. hiding, life

D. gaining, popularity

Now try to match up each of the key words with the passage and see where they fit. You're trying to find synonyms and/or exact replication between the key words in the answer choices and key words in the passage.

A. maintaining – no matches; celebrity – matches in sentences 1, 3, and 5

B. selling – no matches; books – matches with "novels" in sentence 4.

C. hiding – no matches; life – no matches

D. gaining – no matches; popularity –matches with "celebrity" in sentences 1, 3, and 5, because they can be synonyms

At this point there are only two choices that have more than one match, choices A and D, and they both have the same number of matches, and with the same word in the passage, which is the word "celebrity" in the passage. This is a good sign, because CAAP will often write two answer choices that are close. Having two answer choices pointing towards the same key word is a strong indicator that those key words hold the "key" to finding the right answer.

Now let's compare choice A and D and the unmatched key words. Choice A still has "maintaining" which doesn't have a clear match, while choice D has "gaining" which doesn't have a clear match. While neither of those have clear matches in the passage, ask yourself what are the best arguments that would support any kind of connection with either of those two words.

"Maintaining" makes sense when you consider that Twain was interested in tracking his press coverage and that he was actively managing the "spin" of certain stories.

"Gaining" makes sense when you consider that Twain was actively issuing his own press releases, however one key point to remember is that he was only issuing these press releases after another story was already in existence.

Since Twain's press releases were not being released in a news vacuum, but rather as a response mechanism to ensure control over the angle of a story, his releases were more to *maintain* control over his image, rather than *gain* an image in the first place.

Furthermore, when comparing the terms "popularity" and "celebrity", there are similarities between the words, but in referring back to the passage, it is clear that "celebrity" has a stronger connection to the passage, being the exact word used three times in the passage.

Since "celebrity" has a stronger match than "popularity" and "maintaining" makes more sense than "gaining," it is clear that choice A is correct.

2. Use a process of elimination.

A. maintaining his celebrity – The passage discusses how Mark Twain was both aware of his celebrity status and would take steps to ensure that he got the proper coverage in any news story and maintained the image he desired. This is the correct answer.

B. selling more of his books – Mark Twain's novels are mentioned for their popularity and while common sense would dictate that he would be interested in selling more of his books, the passage makes no mention of him doing anything to promote sales.

C. hiding his private life – While the passage demonstrates that Mark Twain was keenly interested in how the public viewed his life, it does not indicate that he cared about hiding his private life, not even mentioning his life outside of the public eye. The passage deals with how he was seen by the public.

D. gaining popularity – At first, this sounds like a good answer choice, because Mark Twain's popularity is mentioned several times. The main difference though is that he wasn't trying to gain popularity, but simply ensuring that the popularity he had was not distorted by bad press.

Sample Question from the Mathematics Test:

Three coins are tossed up in the air. What is the probability that two of them will land heads and one will land tails?

A. 0
B. 1/8
C. 1/4
D. 3/8
E. 1/2

Let's look at a few different methods and steps to solving this problem.

1. Reduction and Division

Quickly eliminate the probabilities that you immediately know. You know to roll all heads is a 1/8 probability, and to roll all tails is a 1/8 probability. Since there are in total 8/8 probabilities, you can subtract those two out, leaving you with 8/8 – 1/8 – 1/8 = 6/8. So after eliminating the possibilities of getting all heads or all tails, you're left with 6/8 probability. Because there are only three coins, all other combinations are going to involve one of either head or tail, and two of the other. All other combinations will either be 2 heads and 1 tail, or 2 tails and 1 head. Those remaining combinations both have the same chance of occurring, meaning that you can just cut the remaining 6/8 probability in half, leaving you with a 3/8ths chance that there will be 2 heads and 1 tail, and another 3/8ths chance that there will be 2 tails and 1 head, making choice D correct.

2. Run Through the Possibilities for that Outcome

You know that you have to have two heads and one tail for the three coins. There are only so many combinations, so quickly run through them all.

You could have:

H, H, H

H, H, T

H, T, H

T, H, H

T, T, H

T, H, T

H, T, T

T, T, T

Reviewing these choices, you can see that three of the eight have two heads and one tail, making choice D correct.

3. Fill in the Blanks with Symbology and Odds

Many probability problems can be solved by drawing blanks on a piece of scratch paper (or making mental notes) for each object used in the problem, then filling in probabilities and multiplying them out. In this case, since there are three coins being flipped, draw three blanks. In the first blank, put an "H" and over it write "1/2". This represents the case where the first coin is flipped as heads. In that case (where the first coin comes up heads), one of the other two coins must come up tails and one must come up heads to fulfill the criteria posed in the problem (2 heads and 1 tail). In the second blank, put a "1" or "1/1". This is because it doesn't matter what is flipped for the second coin, so long as the first coin is heads. In the third blank, put a "1/2". This is because the third coin must be the exact opposite of whatever is in the second blank. Half the time the third coin will be the same as the second coin, and half the time the third coin will be the opposite, hence the "1/2".

Now multiply out the odds. There is a half chance that the first coin will come up "heads", then it doesn't matter for the second coin, then there is a half chance that the third coin will be the opposite of the second coin, which will give the desired result of 2 heads and 1 tail. So, that gives 1/2*1/1*1/2 = 1/4.

But, now you must calculate the probabilities that result if the first coin is flipped tails. So draw another group of three blanks. In the first blank, put a "T" and over it write "1/2". This represents the case where the first coin is flipped as tails. In that case (where the first coin comes up tails), both of the other two coins must come up heads to fulfill the criteria posed in the problem. In the second blank, put an "H" and over it write "1/2". In the third blank, put an "H" and over it write "1/2". Now multiply out the odds. There is a half chance that the first coin will come up "tails", then there is a half chance that the second coin will be heads, and a half chance that the third coin will be heads. So, that gives 1/2*1/2*1/2 = 1/8.

Now, add those two probabilities together. If you flip heads with the first coin, there is a 1/4 chance of ultimately meeting the problem's criteria. If you flip tails with the first coin, there is a 1/8 chance of ultimately meeting the problem's criteria. So, that gives 1/4 + 1/8 = 2/8 + 1/8 = 3/8, which makes choice D correct.

Sample Question from the English Test:

Choose which of four ways of writing the underlined part of the sentence is correct.

<u>While a leader, one can decide</u> to allow the group to determine its course by a simple vote of majority, or we can choose to guide the group without allowing the opportunity for discussion.

A. NO CHANGE
B. While leaders, we can decide
C. While a leader, we can decide
D. While leaders, one can decide

Let's look at a couple of different methods and steps to solving this problem.

1. Agreement in Pronoun Number

All pronouns have to agree in number to their antecedent or noun that they are representing. In the underlined portion, the pronoun "one" has as its antecedent the noun "leader".

Go through and match up each of the pronouns in the answer choices with their antecedents.

A. leader, one – correctly matches singular antecedent to singular pronoun
B. leaders, we – correctly matches plural antecedent to plural pronoun
C. leader, we – incorrectly matches singular antecedent to plural pronoun
D. leaders, one – incorrectly matches plural antecedent to singular pronoun

Based on pronoun number agreement, you can eliminate choices C and D from consideration, because they fail the test.

2. Parallelism

Not only do the pronouns and antecedents in the underlined portion of the sentence have to be correct, but the rest of the sentence has to match as well. The remainder of the sentence has to be parallel to the underlined portion. Part of the sentence that is not underlined has the phrase "we can choose." Notice how this phrase uses the plural pronoun "we". This means that the underlined portion of the sentence has to be plural to agree with the rest of the sentence and have matching plural pronouns and nouns as well.

Quickly review the answer choices and look for whether the nouns and pronouns in the answer choices are singular or plural.

A. leader, one – singular noun, singular pronoun
B. leaders, we – plural noun, plural pronoun
C. leader, we – singular noun, plural pronoun
D. leaders, one – plural noun, singular pronoun

Only choice B has both a plural noun and a plural pronoun, making choice B correct.

Sample Question from the Science Test:

Table 1

Length of 0.10 mm diameter aluminum wire(m)	Resistance (ohms) at 20° C
1	3.55
2	7.10
4	14.20
10	35.50

Based on the information in Table 1, one would predict that a 20 m length of aluminum wire with a 0.10 mm diameter would have a resistance of:

A. 16 ohms
B. 25 ohms
C. 34 ohms
D. 71 ohms

Let's look at a few different methods and steps to solving this problem.

1. Create a Proportion or Ratio

The first way you could approach this problem is by setting up a proportion or ratio. You will find that many of the problems on the ACT can be solved using this simple technique. Usually whenever you have a given pair of numbers (this number goes with that number) and you are given a third number and asked to find what number would be its match, then you have a problem that can be converted into an easy proportion or ratio.

In this case you can take any of the pairs of numbers from Table 1. As an example, let's choose the second set of numbers (2 m and 7.10 ohms).

Form a question with the information you have at your disposal: 2 meters goes to 7.10 ohms as 20 meters (from the question) goes to which resistance?

From your ratio: 2m/7.10 ohms = 20m/x
"x" is used as the missing number that you will solve for.

Cross multiplication provides us with 2*x = 7.10*20 or 2x = 142.

Dividing both sides by 2 gives us 2x/2 = 142/2 or x = 71, making choice D correct.

2. Use Algebra

While you might think that creating an algebra problem is the last thing that you would want to do, it actually can make the problem extremely simple.

The question is asking for the resistance of a 20 m length of wire. The resistance is a function of the length of the wire, so you know that you could probably set up an algebra problem that would have 20 multiplied by some factor "x" that would give you your answer.

So, now you have 20*x = ?

But what exactly is "x"? If 20*x would give you the resistance of a 20 meter piece of wire, than 1*x would give you the resistance of a 1 meter piece of wire. Remember though, the table already told you the resistance of a 1 meter piece of wire – it's 3.55 ohms.

So, if 1*x = 3.55 ohms, then solving for "x" gives you x = 3.55 ohms.

Plugging your solution for "x" back into your initial equation of 20*x = ?, you now have 20*3.55 ohms = 71 ohms, making choice D correct.

3. Look for a Pattern

Much of the time you can get by with just looking for patterns on problems that provide you with a lot of different numbers. In this case, consider the provided table.

1 – 3.55
2 – 7.10
4 – 14.20
10 – 35.50

What patterns do you see in the above number sequences. It appears that when the number in the first column doubled from 1 to 2, the numbers in the second column doubled as well, going from 3.55 to 7.10. Further inspection shows that when the numbers in the first column doubled from 2 to 4, the numbers in the second column doubled again, going from 7.10 to 14.20. Now you've got a pattern, when the first column of numbers doubles, so does the second column.

Since the question asked about a resistance of 20, you should recognize that 20 is the double of 10. Since a length of 10 meant a resistance of 35.50 ohms, then doubling the length of 10 should double the resistance, making 71 ohms, or choice

D, correct.

4. Use Logic

A method that works even faster than finding patterns or setting up equations is using simple logic. It appears that as the first number (the length of the wire) gets larger, so does the second number (the resistance).

Since the length of 10 (the largest length wire in the provided table) has a corresponding resistance of 35.50, then another length (such as 20 in the question) should have a length greater than 35.50. As you inspect the answer choices, there is only one answer choice that is greater than 35.50, which is choice D, making it correct.

Sample Topic for the Writing Test:

What is the most important thing in your life? Discuss why?

Let's look at a few different methods and steps to solving this problem.

1. What's the goal?

Remember that on the essay portion of the CAAP, there isn't a "correct" answer. The answer you choose to give to the topic provided does not have to be the first thing that comes to your mind.

For example, with this topic, your first thought might be your home or car, which are necessary for the basic functions of life, such as providing a roof over your head and a method of transportation. Yet, what would be your supporting answer as to why you would pick your car? Some possibilities might be: "it gets me where I need to go, it is brand new, it is expensive, I like it a lot, it would be difficult to replace, it's shiny."

These answer choices may fill up some space, but don't have much meaning. There are probably things in your life that have much more meaning and priority in other ways that would be better to write about.

The goal is to think of something that has meaning beyond the mere basics of shelter or transportation. You want a topic that you could potentially write pages and pages about, filling each of them with depths of passionate detail. While you probably won't have time to write pages and pages, it's good to have a topic that has plenty of room to be expanded upon.

2. Make a Short List

The best way to think of a good topic would be to create a short list of possibilities.

What are some alternative things that you have that are important? What are things that you would regret and miss for years to come? Perhaps your family, your friends, a relationship, or your faith would be better choices.

After you've made your list, look back over it and see which choice you could write the most information about. That is the one you want to choose.

3. Answer "Why"

Notice that choosing a topic and writing about it does not completely answer the topic question. There are two little words hidden at the back of the initial question, "Discuss why?"

You have to answer that all-important question. If you wrote a sentence as part of your response and one of the essay scorer looked over your shoulder and said, "but why?" would your next sentence answer their question.

For example, suppose you wrote, "The relationship that I have with my father has a lot of meaning."

If someone asked, "But why?" would your next sentence answer It.

Your next sentence should say, "The relationship has meaning because he was there to support me when my mother died. We depended upon each other to get through that period, which was extremely difficult."

Answering the question posed is crucial to your success at writing a great essay. It doesn't do any good to write a good essay if it doesn't answer the question.

Sample Question from the Critical Thinking Test:

The cost of producing radios in Country Q is ten percent less than the cost of producing radios in Country Y. Even after transportation fees and tariff charges are added, it is still cheaper for a company to import radios from Country Q to Country Y than to produce radios in Country Y. The statements above, if true, best support which of the following assertions?

A. Labor costs in Country Q are ten percent below those in Country Y.
B. Importing radios from Country Q to Country Y will eliminate ten percent of the manufacturing jobs in Country Y.
C. The tariff on a radio imported from Country Q to Country Y is less than ten percent of the cost of manufacturing the radio in Country Y.
D. The fee for transporting a radio from Country Q to Country Y is more than ten percent of the cost of manufacturing the radio in Country Q.

Let's look at a couple of different methods of solving this problem.

1. Eliminate Choices

When in doubt, eliminate what you can first. Go through each answer choice and see if you can eliminate it from consideration.

Answer choice A mentions labor costs, although labor costs are not even mentioned in the question. Rarely will CAAP try to trick you by bringing up an unmentioned variable, therefore answer choice A can be eliminated.

Answer choice B mentions manufacturing jobs which wasn't mentioned in the question, and can be eliminated.

Now you're down to just answer choice C and D, making your task much easier.

Answer choice D states that the transportation fee is more than ten percent of the cost of manufacturing the radio. However, if that were true, then the total cost of importing a radio from Country Q would exceed the manufacturing cost in Country Y, making choice D incorrect, because the question clearly states that the importing cost is still less, even after the transportation and tariff costs are added in.

This makes answer choice C the default correct answer.

2. Plug and Chug

Take some sample numbers and plug them into the problem. Rather than having to remember the relationships, writing them down with real numbers helps a lot of students understand the problem better. Use round number like 100 that are easy to use in calculations, especially with percents.

In this case, you could write:

Country Y - $100 is the cost to produce 1 radio
Country Q - $90 is the cost to produce 1 radio (10% less)

The question states that even if transportation fees and tariff charges are added to the cost of producing radios in Country Q, radios are still cheaper to import. Since that would mean that the total cost from Country Q could not exceed $100 (the cost in Country Y), then the transportation and tariff costs could not exceed $10, because the manufacturing cost is already $90, and $90 + any number greater than $10 would exceed $100.

Since the upper limit of the transportation and tariff costs of $10 is 10% of $100, that means that the tariff costs alone would definitely have to be less than 10%, which makes answer choice C correct.

Special Report: How to Overcome Your Fear of Math

If this article started by saying "Math," many of us would feel a shiver crawl up our spines, just by reading that simple word. Images of torturous years in those crippling desks of the math classes can become so vivid to our consciousness that we can almost smell those musty textbooks, and see the smudges of the #2 pencils on our fingers.

If you are still a student, feeling the impact of these sometimes overwhelming classroom sensations, you are not alone if you get anxious at just the thought of taking that compulsory math course. Does your heart beat just that much faster when you have to split the bill for lunch among your friends with a group of your friends? Do you truly believe that you simply don't have the brain for math? Certainly you're good at other things, but math just simply isn't one of them? Have you ever avoided activities, or other school courses because they appear to involve mathematics, with which you're simply not comfortable?

If any one or more of these "symptoms" can be applied to you, you could very well be suffering from a very real condition called "Math Anxiety."

It's not at all uncommon for people to think that they have some sort of math disability or allergy, when in actuality, their block is a direct result of the way in which they were taught math!

In the late 1950's with the dawning of the space age, New Math - a new "fuzzy math" reform that focuses on higher-order thinking, conceptual understanding and solving problems - took the country by storm. It's now becoming ever more clear that teachers were not supplied with the correct, practical and effective way in which they should be teaching new math so that students will understand the methods comfortably. So is it any wonder that so many students struggled so deeply, when their teachers were required to change their entire math systems without the foundation of proper training? Even if you have not been personally, directly affected by that precise event, its impact is still as rampant as ever.

Basically, the math teachers of today are either the teachers who began teaching the new math in the first place (without proper training) or they are the students of the math teachers who taught new math without proper training. Therefore, unless they had a unique, exceptional teacher, their primary, consistent examples of teaching math have been teachers using methods that are not conducive to the general understanding of the entire class. This explains why your discomfort (or fear) of math is not at all rare.

It is very clear why being called up to the chalk board to solve a math problem is such a common example of a terrifying situation for students - and it has very little to do with a fear of being in front of the class. Most of us have had a minimum of one humiliating experience while standing with chalk dusted fingers, with the eyes of every math student piercing through us. These are the images that haunt us all the way through adulthood. But it does not mean that we cannot learn math. It just means that we could be developing a solid case of math anxiety.

But what exactly is math anxiety? It's an very strong emotional sensation of anxiety, panic, or fear that people feel when they think about or must apply their ability to understand mathematics. Sufferers of math anxiety frequently believe that they are incapable of doing activities or taking classes that involve math skills. In fact, some people with math anxiety have developed such a fear that it has become a phobia; aptly named math phobia.

The incidence of math anxiety, especially among college students, but also among high school students, has risen considerably over the last 10 years, and currently this increase shows no signs of slowing down. Frequently students will even chose their college majors and programs based specifically on how little math will be compulsory for the completion of the degree.

The prevalence of math anxiety has become so dramatic on college campuses that many of these schools have special counseling programs that are designed to assist math anxious students to deal with their discomfort and their math problems.

Math anxiety itself is not an intellectual problem, as many people have been lead to believe; it is, in fact, an emotional problem that stems from improper math teaching techniques that have slowly built and reinforced these feelings. However, math anxiety can result in an intellectual problem when its symptoms interfere with a person's ability to learn and understand math.

The fear of math can cause a sort of "glitch" in the brain that can cause an otherwise clever person to stumble over even the simplest of math problems. A study by Dr. Mark H. Ashcraft of Cleveland State University in Ohio showed that college students who usually perform well, but who suffer from math anxiety, will suffer from fleeting lapses in their working memory when they are asked to perform even the most basic mental arithmetic. These same issues regarding memory were not present in the same students when they were required to answer questions that did not involve numbers. This very clearly demonstrated that the memory phenomenon is quite specific to only math.

So what exactly is it that causes this inhibiting math anxiety? Unfortunately it is not as simple as one answer, since math anxiety doesn't have one specific cause.

Frequently math anxiety can result of a student's either negative experience or embarrassment with math or a math teacher in previous years.

These circumstances can prompt the student to believe that he or she is somehow deficient in his or her math abilities. This belief will consistently lead to a poor performance in math tests and courses in general, leading only to confirm the beliefs of the student's inability. This particular phenomenon is referred to as the "self-fulfilling prophecy" by the psychological community. Math anxiety will result in poor performance, rather than it being the other way around.

Dr. Ashcraft stated that math anxiety is a "It's a learned, almost phobic, reaction to math," and that it is not only people prone to anxiety, fear, or panic who can develop math anxiety. The image alone of doing math problems can send the blood pressure and heart rate to race, even in the calmest person.

The study by Dr. Ashcraft and his colleague Elizabeth P. Kirk, discovered that students who suffered from math anxiety were frequently stumped by issues of even the most basic math rules, such as "carrying over" a number, when performing a sum, or "borrowing" from a number when doing a subtraction. Lapses such as this occurred only on working memory questions involving numbers.

To explain the problem with memory, Ashcraft states that when math anxiety begins to take its effect, the sufferer experiences a rush of thoughts, leaving little room for the focus required to perform even the simplest of math problems. He stated that "you're draining away the energy you need for solving the problem by worrying about it."

The outcome is a "vicious cycle," for students who are sufferers of math anxiety. As math anxiety is developed, the fear it promotes stands in the way of learning, leading to a decrease in self-confidence in the ability to perform even simple arithmetic.

A large portion of the problem lies in the ways in which math is taught to students today. In the US, students are frequently taught the rules of math, but rarely will they learn why a specific approach to a math problems work. Should students be provided with a foundation of "deeper understanding" of math, it may prevent the development of phobias.

Another study that was published in the Journal of Experimental Psychology by Dr. Jamie Campbell and Dr. Qilin Xue of the University of Saskatchewan in Saskatoon, Canada, reflected the same concepts. The researchers in this study looked at university students who were educated in Canada and China, discovering that the Chinese students could generally outperform the Canadian-educated students when it came to solving complex math problems involving procedural knowledge - the ability to know how to solve a math problem, instead of simply having ideas memorized.

A portion of this result seemed to be due to the use of calculators within both elementary and secondary schools; while Canadians frequently used them, the Chinese students did not.

However, calculators were not the only issue. Since Chinese-educated students also outperformed Canadian-educated students in complex math, it is suggested that cultural factors may also have an impact. However, the short-cut of using the calculator may hinder the development of the problem solving skills that are key to performing well in math.

Though it is critical that students develop such fine math skills, it is easier said than done. It would involve an overhaul of the training among all elementary and secondary educators, changing the education major in every college.

Math Myths

One problem that contributes to the progression of math anxiety, is the belief of many math myths. These erroneous math beliefs include the following:

Men are better in math than women - however, research has failed to demonstrate that there is any difference in math ability between the sexes. There is a single best way to solve a math problem - however, the majority of math problems can be solved in a number of different ways. By saying that there is only one way to solve a math problem, the thinking and creative skills of the student are held back.

Some people have a math mind, and others do not - in truth, the majority of people have much more potential for their math capabilities than they believe of themselves.

It is a bad thing to count by using your fingers - counting by using fingers has actually shown that an understanding of arithmetic has been established. People who are skilled in math can do problems quickly in their heads - in actuality, even math professors will review their example problems before they teach them in their classes.

The anxieties formed by these myths can frequently be perpetuated by a range of mind games that students seem to play with themselves. These math mind games include the following beliefs:

I don't perform math fast enough - actually everyone has a different rate at which he or she can learn. The speed of the solving of math problems is not important as long as the student can solve it.

I don't have the mind for math - this belief can inhibit a student's belief in him or herself, and will therefore interfere with the student's real ability to learn math.

I got the correct answer, but it was done the wrong way - there is no single best way to complete a math problem. By believing this, a student's creativity and overall understanding of math is hindered.

If I can get the correct answer, then it is too simple - students who suffer from math anxiety frequently belittle their own abilities when it comes to their math capabilities.

Math is unrelated to my "real" life - by freeing themselves of the fear of math, math anxiety sufferers are only limiting their choices and freedoms for the rest of their life.

Fortunately, there are many ways to help those who suffer from math anxiety. Since math anxiety is a learned, psychological response to doing or thinking about math, that interferes with the sufferer's ability to understand and perform math, it is not at all a reflection of the sufferer's true math sills and abilities.

Helpful Strategies

Many strategies and therapies have been developed to help students to overcome their math anxious responses. Some of these helpful strategies include the following:

Reviewing and learning basic arithmetic principles, techniques and methods. Frequently math anxiety is a result of the experience of many students with early negative situations, and these students have never truly developed a strong base in basic arithmetic, especially in the case of multiplication and fractions. Since math is a discipline that is built on an accumulative foundation, where the concepts are built upon gradually from simpler concepts, a student who has not achieved a solid basis in arithmetic will experience difficulty in learning higher order math. Taking a remedial math course, or a short math course that focuses on arithmetic can often make a considerable difference in reducing the anxious response that math anxiety sufferers have with math.

Becoming aware of any thoughts, actions and feelings that are related to math and responses to math. Math anxiety has a different effect on different students. Therefore it is very important to become familiar with any reactions that the math anxiety sufferer may have about him/herself and the situation when math has been encountered. If the sufferer becomes aware of any irrational or unrealistic thoughts, it's possible to better concentrate on replacing these thoughts with more positive and realistic ones.

Find help! Math anxiety, as we've mentioned, is a learned response, that is reinforced repeatedly over a period of time, and is therefore not something that can be eliminated instantaneously. Students can more effectively reduce their anxious responses with the help of many different services that are readily available. Seeking the assistance of a psychologist or counselor, especially one with a specialty in math anxiety, can assist the sufferer in performing an analysis of his/her psychological response to math, as well as learning anxiety management skills, and developing effective coping strategies. Other great tools are tutors, classes that teach better abilities to take better notes in math class, and other math learning aids.

Learning the mathematic vocabulary will instantly provide a better chance for understanding new concepts. One major issue among students is the lack of understanding of the terms and vocabulary that are common jargon within math classes. Typically math classes will utilize words in a completely different way from the way in which they are utilized in all other subjects. Students easily mistake their lack of understanding the math terms with their mathematical abilities.

Learning anxiety reducing techniques and methods for anxiety management. Anxiety greatly interferes with a student's ability to concentrate, think clearly, pay attention, and remember new concepts. When these same students can learn to relax, using anxiety management techniques, the student can regain his or her ability to control his or her emotional and physical symptoms of anxiety that interfere with the capabilities of mental processing.

Working on creating a positive overall attitude about mathematics. Looking at math with a positive attitude will reduce anxiety through the building of a positive attitude.

Learning to self-talk in a positive way. Pep talking oneself through a positive self talk can greatly assist in overcoming beliefs in math myths or the mind games that may be played. Positive self-talking is an effective way to replace the negative thoughts - the ones that create the anxiety. Even if the sufferer doesn't believe the statements at first, it plants a positive seed in the subconscious, and allows a positive outlook to grow.

Beyond this, students should learn effective math class, note taking and studying techniques. Typically, the math anxious students will avoid asking questions to save themselves from embarrassment. They will sit in the back of classrooms, and refrain from seeking assistance from the professor. Moreover, they will put off studying for math until the very last moment, since it causes them such substantial discomfort. Alone, or a combination of these negative behaviors work only to reduce the anxiety of the students, but in reality, they are actually building a substantially more intense anxiety.

There are many different positive behaviors that can be adopted by math anxious students, so that they can learn to better perform within their math classes.

Sit near the front of the class. This way, there will be fewer distractions, and there will be more of a sensation of being a part of the topic of discussion. If any questions arise, ASK! If one student has a question, then there are certain to be others who have the same question but are too nervous to ask - perhaps because they have not yet learned how to deal with their own math anxiety.

Seek extra help from the professor after class or during office hours.

Prepare, prepare, prepare - read textbook material before the class, do the homework and work out any problems available within the textbook. Math skills are developed through practice and repetition, so the more practice and repetition, the better the math skills.

Review the material once again after class, to repeat it another time, and to reinforce the new concepts that were learned.

Beyond these tactics that can be taken by the students themselves, teachers and parents need to know that they can also have a large impact on the reduction of math anxiety within students.

As parents and teachers, there is a natural desire to help students to learn and understand how they will one day utilize different math techniques within their everyday lives. But when the student or teacher displays the symptoms of a person who has had nightmarish memories regarding math, where hesitations then develop in the instruction of students, these fears are automatically picked up by the students and commonly adopted as their own.

However, it is possible for teachers and parents to move beyond their own fears to better educate students by overcoming their own hesitations and learning to enjoy math.

Begin by adopting the outlook that math is a beautiful, imaginative or living thing. Of course, we normally think of mathematics as numbers that can be added or subtracted, multiplied or divided, but that is simply the beginning of it.

By thinking of math as something fun and imaginative, parents and teachers can teach children different ways to manipulate numbers, for example in balancing a checkbook. Parents rarely tell their children that math is everywhere around us; in nature, art, and even architecture. Usually, this is because they were never shown these relatively simple connections. But that pattern can break very simply through the participation of parents and teachers.

The beauty and hidden wonders of mathematics can easily be emphasized through a focus that can open the eyes of students to the incredible mathematical patterns that arise everywhere within the natural world. Observations and discussions can be made into things as fascinating as spider webs, leaf patterns, sunflowers and even coastlines. This makes math not only beautiful, but also inspiring and (dare we say) fun!

Pappas Method

For parents and teachers to assist their students in discovering the true wonders of mathematics, the techniques of Theoni Pappas can easily be applied, as per her popular and celebrated book "Fractals, Googols and Other Mathematical Tales." Pappas used to be a math phobia sufferer and created a fascinating step-by-step program for parents and teachers to use in order to teach students the joy of math.

Her simple, constructive step-by-step program goes as follows:

Don't let your fear of math come across to your kids - Parents must be careful not to perpetuate the mathematical myth - that math is only for specially talented "math types." Strive not to make comments like; "they don't like math" or "I have never been good at math." When children overhear comments like these from their primary role models they begin to dread math before even considering a chance of experiencing its wonders. It is important to encourage your children to read and explore the rich world of mathematics, and to practice mathematics without imparting negative biases.

Don't immediately associate math with computation (counting) - It is very important to realize that math is not just numbers and computations, but a realm of exciting ideas that touch every part of our lives -from making a telephone call to how the hair grows on someone's head. Take your children outside and point out real objects that display math concepts. For example, show them the symmetry of a leaf or angles on a building. Take a close look at the spirals in a spider web or intricate patterns of a snowflake.

Help your child understand why math is important - Math improves problem solving, increases competency and should be applied in different ways. It's the same as reading. You can learn the basics of reading without ever enjoying a novel. But, where's the excitement in that? With math, you could stop with the basics. But why when there is so much more to be gained by a fuller Understanding? Life is so much more enriching when we go beyond the basics. Stretch your children's minds to become involved in mathematics in ways that will not only be practical but also enhance their lives.

Make math as "hands on" as possible - Mathematicians participate in mathematics. To really experience math encourage your child to dig in and tackle problems in creative ways. Help them learn how to manipulate numbers using concrete references they understand as well as things they can see or touch. Look for patterns everywhere, explore shapes and symmetries. How many octagons do you see each day on the way to the grocery store? Play math puzzles and games and then encourage your child to try to invent their own. And, whenever possible, help your child realize a mathematical conclusion with real and tangible results. For example, measure out a full glass of juice with a measuring cup and then ask your child to drink half. Measure what is left. Does it measure half of a cup?

Read books that make math exciting:
Fractals, Googols and Other Mathematical Tales introduces an animated cat who explains fractals, tangrams and other mathematical concepts you've probably

never heard of to children in terms they can understand. This book can double as a great text book by using one story per lesson.

A Wrinkle in Time is a well-loved classic, combining fantasy and science.

The Joy of Mathematics helps adults explore the beauty of mathematics that is all around.

The Math Curse is an amusing book for 4-8 year olds.

The Gnarly Gnews is a free, humorous bi-monthly newsletter on mathematics.

The Phantom Tollbooth is an Alice in Wonderland-style adventure into the worlds of words and numbers.

Use the internet to help your child explore the fascinating world of mathematics.

Web Math provides a powerful set of math-solvers that gives you instant answers to the stickiest problems.

Math League has challenging math materials and contests for fourth grade and above.

Silver Burdett Ginn Mathematics offers Internet-based math activities for grades K-6.

The Gallery of Interactive Geometry is full of fascinating, interactive geometry activities.

Math is very much like a language of its own. And like any second language, it will get rusty if it is not practiced enough. For that reason, students should always be looking into new ways to keep understanding and brushing up on their math skills, to be certain that foundations do not crumble, inhibiting the learning of new levels of math.

There are many different books, services and websites that have been developed to take the fear out of math, and to help even the most uncertain student develop self confidence in his or her math capabilities.

There is no reason for math or math classes to be a frightening experience, nor should it drive a student crazy, making them believe that they simply don't have the "math brain" that is needed to solve certain problems.

There are friendly ways to tackle such problems and it's all a matter of dispelling myths and creating a solid math foundation.

Concentrate on re-learning the basics and feeling better about yourself in math, and you'll find that the math brain you've always wanted, was there all along.

Secret Key #1 – Time is Your Greatest Enemy

To succeed on the CAAP, you must use your time wisely. Many students do not finish at least one section. The table below shows the time challenge you are faced with:

SECTION	Total amount of time allotted	Number of questions	Time to answer each question
Reading	40 min	36	1.11 min
Writing Skills	40 min	72	.56 min
Writing Essay	40 min	2	20 min
Mathematics	40 min	35	1.14 min
Science	40 min	45	.89
Critical Thinking	40 min	32	1.25

As you can see, the time constraints are brutal. To succeed, you must ration your time properly.

On the some sections, the test is separated into passages. The reason that time is so critical is that 1) every question counts the same toward your final score, and 2) the passages are not in order of difficulty. If you have to rush during the last passage, then you will miss out on answering easier questions correctly. It is natural to want to pause and figure out the hardest questions, but you must resist the temptation and move quickly.

Success Strategy #1

Pace Yourself

Wear a watch to the CAAP Test. At the beginning of the test, check the time (or start a chronometer on your watch to count the minutes), and check the time after each passage or every few questions to make sure you are "on schedule."

Remember that on most sections you have a little less or close to a minute per question, which makes it easy to keep track of your time.

If you find that you are falling behind time during the test, begin skipping difficult questions (unless you know it at a quick glance). Once you catch back up, you can continue working each problem. If you have time at the end, go back then and finish the questions that you left behind.

If you are forced to speed up, do it efficiently. Usually one or more answer choices can be eliminated without too much difficulty. Above all, don't panic. Don't speed up and just begin guessing at random choices. By pacing yourself, and continually monitoring your progress against the clock or your watch, you will always know exactly how far ahead or behind you are with your available time. If you find that you are one minute behind on a section, don't skip a question without spending any time on it, just to catch back up. Spend perhaps 45 seconds on the next question and after four questions, you will have caught back up more gradually. Once you catch back up, you can continue working each problem at your normal pace.

Furthermore, don't dwell on the problems that you were rushed on. If a problem was taking up too much time and you made a hurried guess, it must be difficult. The difficult questions are the ones you are most likely to miss anyway, so it isn't a big loss. It is better to end with more time than you need than to run out of time. You can always go back and work the problems that you skipped. If you have time left over, as you review the skipped questions, start at the earliest skipped question, spend at most another minute, and then move on to the next skipped question.

Lastly, sometimes it is beneficial to slow down if you are constantly getting ahead of time. You are always more likely to catch a careless mistake by working more slowly than quickly, and among very high-scoring students (those who are likely to have lots of time left over), careless errors affect the score more than mastery of material.

Scanning

For Reading passages, don't waste time reading, enjoying, and completely understanding the passage. Simply scan the passage to get a rough idea of what it is about. You will return to the passage for each question, so there is no need to memorize it. Only spend as much time scanning as is necessary to get a vague impression of its overall subject content.

Secret Key #2 – Guessing is not Guesswork

You probably know that guessing is a good idea on the CAAP- unlike other standardized tests, there is no penalty for getting a wrong answer. Even if you have no idea about a question, you still have a 20-25% chance of getting it right.

Most students do not understand the impact that proper guessing can have on their score. Unless you score extremely high, guessing will significantly contribute to your final score.

Monkeys Take the CAAP

What most students don't realize is that to insure that 20-25% chance, you have to guess randomly. If you put 20 monkeys in a room to take the CAAP, assuming they answered once per question and behaved themselves, on average they would get 20-25% of the questions correct. Put 20 students in the room, and the average will be much lower among guessed questions. Why?

1. CAAP intentionally writes deceptive answer choices that "look" right. A student has no idea about a question, so picks the "best looking" answer, which is often wrong. The monkey has no idea what looks good and what doesn't, so will consistently be lucky about 20-25% of the time.
2. Students will eliminate answer choices from the guessing pool based on a hunch or intuition. Simple but correct answers often get excluded, leaving a 0% chance of being correct. The monkey has no clue, and often gets lucky with the best choice.

This is why the process of elimination endorsed by most test courses is flawed and detrimental to your performance- students don't guess, they make an ignorant stab in the dark that is usually worse than random.

Success Strategy #2

Let me introduce one of the most valuable ideas of this course- the $5 challenge:

You only mark your "best guess" if you are willing to bet $5 on it.
You only eliminate choices from guessing if you are willing to bet $5 on it.

Why $5? Five dollars is an amount of money that is small yet not insignificant, and can really add up fast (20 questions could cost you $100). Likewise, each answer choice on one question of the CAAP will have a small impact on your overall score, but it can really add up to a lot of points in the end.

The process of elimination IS valuable. The following shows your chance of guessing it right:

If you eliminate this many choices:	0	1	2	3	4
Chance of getting it correct	20%	25%	33%	50%	100%

However, if you accidentally eliminate the right answer or go on a hunch for an incorrect answer, your chances drop dramatically: to 0%. By guessing among all the answer choices, you are GUARANTEED to have a shot at the right answer.

That's why the $5 test is so valuable- if you give up the advantage and safety of a pure guess, it had better be worth the risk.

What we still haven't covered is how to be sure that whatever guess you make is truly random. Here's the easiest way:

Always pick the first answer choice among those remaining.

Such a technique means that you have decided, **before you see a single test question**, exactly how you are going to guess- and since the order of choices tells you nothing about which one is correct, this guessing technique is perfectly random.

Let's try an example-

A student encounters the following problem on the Mathematics test:

What is $(x^2)(x^3)$ equal to?

    A. x^1
    B. x^5
    C. x^6
    D. x^8
    E. x^9

The student has a small idea about this question- he is pretty sure that you are supposed to either add the two exponents (2+3 = 5), or multiply them (2*3 = 6) but he wouldn't bet $5 on either choice. He knows that it isn't any of the other choices and so he is willing to bet $5 on both choices A, D and E not being correct. So he is down to choices B and C. At this point, he guesses 2, since 2 is the first choice remaining.

The student is correct by choosing 2, since $(x^2)(x^3)$ is equal to x^5. He only eliminated those choices he was willing to bet money on, AND he did not let his stale memories (often things not known definitely will get mixed up in the exact opposite arrangement in one's head) about the rules for exponents influence his guess. He blindly chose the first remaining choice, and was rewarded with the fruits of a random guess.

This section is not meant to scare you away from making educated guesses or eliminating choices- you just need to define when a choice is worth eliminating. The $5 test, along with a pre-defined random guessing strategy, is the best way to make sure you reap all of the benefits of guessing.

Summary of Guessing Techniques

1. Eliminate as many choices as you can by using the $5 test. Use the common guessing strategies to help in the elimination process, but only eliminate choices that pass the $5 test.
2. Among the remaining choices, only pick your "best guess" if it passes the $5 test.
3. Otherwise, guess randomly by picking the first remaining choice.

Secret Key #3 – Practice Smarter, Not Harder

Many students delay the test preparation process because they dread the awful amounts of practice time they think necessary to succeed on the test. We have refined an effective method that will take you only a fraction of the time.

There are a number of "obstacles" in your way on the CAAP. Among these are answering questions, finishing in time, and mastering test-taking strategies. All must be executed on the day of the test at peak performance, or your score will suffer. The CAAP is a mental marathon that has a large impact on your future.

Just like a marathon runner, it is important to work your way up to the full challenge. So first you just worry about questions, and then time, and finally strategy:

Success Strategy #3

1. Find a good source for CAAP practice tests. If you are willing to make a larger time investment, consider using more than one study guide- often the different approaches of multiple authors will help you "get" difficult concepts.
2. Take a practice test with no time constraints, with all study helps "open book." Take your time with questions and focus on applying the strategies.
3. Take another test, this time with time constraints, with all study helps "open book."
4. Take a final practice test with no open material and time limits.

If you have time to take more practice tests, just repeat step 5. By gradually exposing yourself to the full rigors of the test environment, you will condition your mind to the stress of test day and maximize your success.

Secret Key #4 – Prepare, Don't Procrastinate

Let me state an obvious fact: if you take the CAAP three times, you will get three different scores. This is due to the way you feel on test day, the level of preparedness you have, and, despite claims to the contrary, some tests WILL be easier for you than others.

Since your future depends so much on your score, you should maximize your chances of success. In order to maximize the likelihood of success, you've got to prepare in advance. This means taking practice tests and spending time learning the information and test taking strategies you will need to succeed.

The first time you take the CAAP, don't take it as a "practice" test. Feel free to take sample tests on your own, but when you go to take the CAAP, be prepared, be focused, and do your best the first time!

Secret Key #5 – Test Yourself

Everyone knows that time is money. There is no need to spend too much of your time or too little of your time preparing for the CAAP. You should only spend as much of your precious time preparing as is necessary for you to pass it.

Success Strategy

Once you have taken a practice test under real conditions of time constraints, then you will know if you are ready for the test or not.

If you have scored extremely high the first time that you take a practice test, then there is not much point in spending countless hours studying. You are already there.

Benchmark your abilities by retaking practice tests and seeing how much you have improved. Once you score high enough, then you are ready.

If you have scored well below where you need, then knuckle down and begin studying in earnest. Check your improvement regularly through the use of practice tests under real conditions. Above all, don't worry, panic, or give up. The key is perseverance!

Then, when you go to take the CAAP, remain confident and remember how well you did on the practice tests. If you can score a passing score on a practice test, then you can do the same on the real thing.

General Strategies

The most important thing you can do is to ignore your fears and jump into the test immediately- do not be overwhelmed by any strange-sounding terms. You have to jump into the test like jumping into a pool- all at once is the easiest way.

Make Predictions

As you read and understand the question, try to guess what the answer will be. Remember that several of the answer choices are wrong, and once you begin reading them, your mind will immediately become cluttered with answer choices designed to throw you off. Your mind is typically the most focused immediately after you have read the question and digested its contents. If you can, try to predict what the correct answer will be. You may be surprised at what you can predict.

Quickly scan the choices and see if your prediction is in the listed answer choices. If it is, then you can be quite confident that you have the right answer. It still won't hurt to check the other answer choices, but most of the time, you've got it!

Answer the Question

It may seem obvious to only pick answer choices that answer the question, but the test writers can create some excellent answer choices that are wrong. Don't pick an answer just because it sounds right, or you believe it to be true. It MUST answer the question. Once you've made your selection, always go back and check it against the question and make sure that you didn't misread the question, and the answer choice does answer the question posed.

Benchmark

After you read the first answer choice, decide if you think it sounds correct or not. If it doesn't, move on to the next answer choice. If it does, mentally mark that answer choice. This doesn't mean that you've definitely selected it as your answer choice, it just means that it's the best you've seen thus far. Go ahead and read the next choice. If the next choice is worse than the one you've already selected, keep going to the next answer choice. If the next choice is better than the choice you've already selected, mentally mark the new answer choice as your best guess.

The first answer choice that you select becomes your standard. Every other answer choice must be benchmarked against that standard. That choice is correct until proven otherwise by another answer choice beating it out. Once you've decided that no other answer choice seems as good, do one final check to ensure that your answer choice answers the question posed.

Valid Information

Don't discount any of the information provided in the question. Every piece of information may be necessary to determine the correct answer. None of the information in the question is there to throw you off (while the answer choices will certainly have information to throw you off). If two seemingly unrelated topics are discussed, don't ignore either. You can be confident there is a relationship, or it wouldn't be included in the question, and you are probably going to have to determine what is that relationship to find the answer.

Avoid "Fact Traps"

Don't get distracted by a choice that is factually true. Your search is for the answer that answers the question. Stay focused and don't fall for an answer that is true but incorrect. Always go back to the question and make sure you're choosing an answer that actually answers the question and is not just a true statement. An answer can be factually correct, but it MUST answer the question asked. Additionally, two answers can both be seemingly correct, so be sure to read all of the answer choices, and make sure that you get the one that BEST answers the question.

Milk the Question

Some of the questions may throw you completely off. They might deal with a subject you have not been exposed to, or one that you haven't reviewed in years. While your lack of knowledge about the subject will be a hindrance, the question itself can give you many clues that will help you find the correct answer. Read the question carefully and look for clues. Watch particularly for adjectives and nouns describing difficult terms or words that you don't recognize. Regardless of if you completely understand a word or not, replacing it with a synonym either provided or one you more familiar with may help you to understand what the questions are asking. Rather than wracking your mind about specific detailed information concerning a difficult term or word, try to use mental substitutes that are easier to understand.

The Trap of Familiarity

Don't just choose a word because you recognize it. On difficult questions, you may not recognize a number of words in the answer choices. The test writers don't put "make-believe" words on the test; so don't think that just because you only recognize all the words in one answer choice means that answer choice must be correct. If you only recognize words in one answer choice, then focus on that one. Is it correct? Try your best to determine if it is correct. If it is, that is great, but if it doesn't, eliminate it. Each word and answer choice you eliminate increases your chances of getting the question correct, even if you then have to guess among the unfamiliar choices.

Eliminate Answers

Eliminate choices as soon as you realize they are wrong. But be careful! Make sure you consider all of the possible answer choices. Just because one appears right, doesn't mean that the next one won't be even better! The test writers will usually put more than one good answer choice for every question, so read all of them. Don't worry if you are stuck between two that seem right. By getting down to just two remaining possible choices, your odds are now 50/50. Rather than wasting too much time, play the odds. You are guessing, but guessing wisely, because you've been able to knock out some of the answer choices that you know are wrong. If you are eliminating choices and realize that the last answer choice you are left with is also obviously wrong, don't panic. Start over and consider each choice again. There may easily be something that you missed the first time and will realize on the second pass.

Tough Questions

If you are stumped on a problem or it appears too hard or too difficult, don't waste time. Move on! Remember though, if you can quickly check for obviously incorrect answer choices, your chances of guessing correctly are greatly improved. Before you completely give up, at least try to knock out a couple of possible answers. Eliminate what you can and then guess at the remaining answer choices before moving on.

Brainstorm

If you get stuck on a difficult question, spend a few seconds quickly brainstorming. Run through the complete list of possible answer choices. Look at each choice and ask yourself, "Could this answer the question satisfactorily?" Go through each answer choice and consider it independently of the other. By systematically going through all possibilities, you may find something that you would otherwise overlook. Remember that when you get stuck, it's important to try to keep moving.

Read Carefully

Understand the problem. Read the question and answer choices carefully. Don't miss the question because you misread the terms. You have plenty of time to read each question thoroughly and make sure you understand what is being asked. Yet a happy medium must be attained, so don't waste too much time. You must read carefully, but efficiently.

Face Value

When in doubt, use common sense. Always accept the situation in the problem at face value. Don't read too much into it. These problems will not require you to make huge leaps of logic. The test writers aren't trying to throw you off with a cheap trick. If you have to go beyond creativity and make a leap of logic in order to have an answer choice answer the question, then you should look at the other answer choices. Don't overcomplicate the problem by creating theoretical relationships or explanations that will warp time or space. These are normal problems rooted in reality. It's just that the applicable relationship or explanation may not be readily apparent and you have to figure things out. Use your common sense to interpret anything that isn't clear.

Prefixes

If you're having trouble with a word in the question or answer choices, try dissecting it. Take advantage of every clue that the word might include. Prefixes and suffixes can be a huge help. Usually they allow you to determine a basic meaning. Pre- means before, post- means after, pro - is positive, de- is negative. From these prefixes and suffixes, you can get an idea of the general meaning of the word and try to put it into context. Beware though of any traps. Just because con is the opposite of pro, doesn't necessarily mean congress is the opposite of progress!

Hedge Phrases

Watch out for critical "hedge" phrases, such as likely, may, can, will often, sometimes, often, almost, mostly, usually, generally, rarely, sometimes. Question writers insert these hedge phrases to cover every possibility. Often an answer choice will be wrong simply because it leaves no room for exception. Avoid answer choices that have definitive words like "exactly," and "always".

Switchback Words

Stay alert for "switchbacks". These are the words and phrases frequently used to alert you to shifts in thought. The most common switchback word is "but". Others include although, however, nevertheless, on the other hand, even though, while, in spite of, despite, regardless of.

New Information

Correct answer choices will rarely have completely new information included. Answer choices typically are straightforward reflections of the material asked about and will directly relate to the question. If a new piece of information is included in an answer choice that doesn't even seem to relate to the topic being asked about, then that answer choice is likely incorrect. All of the information needed to answer the question is usually provided for you, and so you should not have to make guesses that are unsupported or choose answer choices that require unknown information that cannot be reasoned on its own.

Time Management

On technical questions, don't get lost on the technical terms. Don't spend too much time on any one question. If you don't know what a term means, then since you don't have a dictionary, odds are you aren't going to get much further. You should immediately recognize terms as whether or not you know them. If you don't, work with the other clues that you have, the other answer choices and terms provided, but don't waste too much time trying to figure out a difficult term.

Contextual Clues

Look for contextual clues. An answer can be right but not correct. The contextual clues will help you find the answer that is most right and is correct. Understand the context in which a phrase or statement is made. This will help you make important distinctions.

Don't Panic

Panicking will not answer any questions for you. Therefore, it isn't helpful. When you first see the question, if your mind goes blank, take a deep breath. Force yourself to mechanically go through the steps of solving the problem and using the strategies you've learned.

Pace Yourself

Don't get clock fever. It's easy to be overwhelmed when you're looking at a page full of questions, your mind is full of random thoughts and feeling confused, and the clock is ticking down faster than you would like. Calm down and maintain the pace that you have set for yourself. As long as you are on track by monitoring your pace, you are guaranteed to have enough time for yourself. When you get to the last few minutes of the test, it may seem like you won't have enough time left, but if you only have as many questions as you should have left at that point, then you're right on track!

Answer Selection

The best way to pick an answer choice is to eliminate all of those that are wrong, until only one is left and confirm that is the correct answer. Sometimes though, an answer choice may immediately look right. Be careful! Take a second to make sure that the other choices are not equally obvious. Don't make a hasty mistake. There are only two times that you should stop before checking other answers. First is when you are positive that the answer choice you have selected is correct. Second is when time is almost out and you have to make a quick guess!

Check Your Work

Since you will probably not know every term listed and the answer to every question, it is important that you get credit for the ones that you do know. Don't miss any questions through careless mistakes. If at all possible, try to take a second to look back over your answer selection and make sure you've selected the correct answer choice and haven't made a costly careless mistake (such as marking an answer choice that you didn't mean to mark). This quick double check should more than pay for itself in caught mistakes for the time it costs.

Beware of Directly Quoted Answers

Sometimes an answer choice will repeat word for word a portion of the question or reference section. However, beware of such exact duplication – it may be a trap! More than likely, the correct choice will paraphrase or summarize a point, rather than being exactly the same wording.

Slang

Scientific sounding answers are better than slang ones. An answer choice that begins "To compare the outcomes…" is much more likely to be correct than one that begins "Because some people insisted…"

Extreme Statements

Avoid wild answers that throw out highly controversial ideas that are proclaimed as established fact. An answer choice that states the "process should be used in certain situations, if…" is much more likely to be correct than one that states the "process should be discontinued completely." The first is a calm rational statement and doesn't even make a definitive, uncompromising stance, using a hedge word "if" to provide wiggle room, whereas the second choice is a radical idea and far more extreme.

Answer Choice Families

When you have two or more answer choices that are direct opposites or parallels, one of them is usually the correct answer. For instance, if one answer choice states "x increases" and another answer choice states "x decreases" or "y increases," then those two or three answer choices are very similar in construction and fall into the same family of answer choices. A family of answer choices is when two or three answer choices are very similar in construction, and yet often have a directly opposite meaning. Usually the correct answer choice will be in that family of answer choices. The "odd man out" or answer choice that doesn't seem to fit the parallel construction of the other answer choices is more likely to be incorrect.

Special Report: Additional Bonus Material

Due to our efforts to try to keep this book to a manageable length, we've created a link that will give you access to all of your additional bonus material.

Please visit http://www.mometrix.com/bonus948/caap to access the information.